"There are more things in heaven and earth...
than are dreamt of in your philosophy."
—Hamlet (to his skeptical friend, Horatio)

"To a very advanced race we might appear as such
a primitive life form as to represent delightful pets,
interesting experimental animals, or a gourmet
delicacy."
—official NASA memorandum

Almanac of ALIEN Encounters

by Eric Elfman

illustrated by Jeff Westover

Random House 🏠 New York

Interior photographs: Fortean Picture Library, pp. 12, 23, 27, 44 (both), 62, 111, 112; NASA, p. 160; NASA/NSSDC, pp. 94 (both), 114 (both).

www.randomhouse.com/kids

Visit author Eric Elfman at www.elfmanworld.com

Library of Congress Cataloging-in-Publication Data
Elfman, Eric.
Almanac of alien encounters / by Eric Elfman ; illustrated by Jeff Westover.
p. cm. Includes bibliographical references and index.
ISBN 0-679-87288-4 (trade) — ISBN 0-679-97288-9 (lib. bdg.)
1. Unidentified flying objects—Sightings and encounters—Juvenile literature.
[1. Unidentified flying objects.] I. Westover, Jeff, ill. II. Title.
TL789.2 .E44 2001 001.942—dc21 00-037298

Printed in the United States of America
June 2001 10 9 8 7 6 5 4 3 2 1

For Jan, my favorite skeptic —E.E.

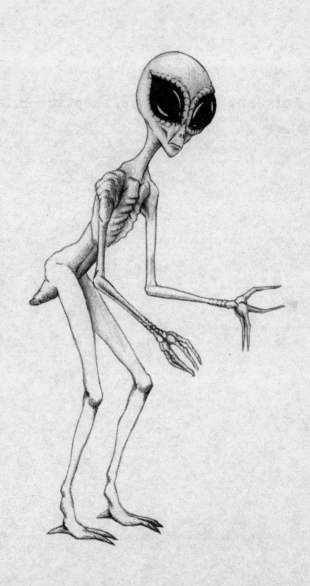

contents

Introduction

Consider, if you will, the following:

The District Attorney of Sacramento and California's Secretary of State, along with hundreds of other people, watch an object cruise through the night sky, shining searchlights at the ground—a good *seven* years before the Wright Brothers fly the first airplane at Kitty Hawk.

A police officer in New Mexico approaches two children standing beside a disabled vehicle on the side of the road. Upon closer inspection, the officer sees that the two children are in fact two small humanoid beings standing beside an egg-shaped metallic craft. The beings make a hasty retreat back into their craft, which then shoots into the sky, trailing flames.

For a period of eight months, military personnel at bases across the United States report unidentified objects violating the airspace over their installations and missile silos. After months of investigation, some Air Force officials are convinced an alien invasion is imminent.

Are these stories true? Yes. Did the people involved encounter alien beings from other planets? Maybe. Can such incidents be explained in other ways? Usually.

It's confusing.

There's no question that most people who believe they have seen aliens and/or their crafts were in fact fooled by ordinary objects such as weather balloons, airplanes, planets, and stars. And there's no doubt that many folks with similar claims are deluded or are simply seeking attention. Of course, it's also possible that our planet is sometimes visited by aliens.

Most astronomers, after all, believe that our universe absolutely teems with life forms. Some estimate that our galaxy alone may hold as many as 10 billion planets capable of supporting life. Even if only some small percentage of those 10 billion planets are inhabited by *intelligent* life forms, it doesn't seem wildly far-fetched to assume that a fraction of those support civilizations more advanced than our own.

Nevertheless, most scientists—even those who believe in the probability of life on other planets—scoff at the notion that aliens are visiting Earth. The vast distances between the stars make such travel impossible, they say. Interstellar voyages would take thousands of years and consume unimaginably large amounts of fuel.

And yet, people—sometimes highly reliable people—keep seeing really strange stuff in the sky. What gives?

In this book you will read about UFO sightings throughout history, encounters with aliens, reports of crashed flying saucers, and numerous other improbable-sounding phenomena. You'll learn about government cover-ups, deliberate hoaxes, and alternative theories for the existence of UFOs. You'll also read the scientific explanations offered by skeptics for these remarkable events and sightings.

Ultimately, you'll have to decide for yourself who and what to believe.

And in the end, although the mystery may be no nearer to a solution, you'll no doubt agree that it is, indeed, a mystery.

ET TERM: "EXTRA-TERRESTRIAL"

"Extra" means "outside of" or "beyond." "Terrestrial" (tuh-RESS-tree-ul) means "of the Earth." "Extra-terrestrial" (or "ET," for short) means "outside of the Earth."

THE SPECTRUM OF BELIEF

People who research and investigate alien encounters include scientists, military personnel, writers, filmmakers, witnesses, abductees, and curious citizens from all walks of life. Their opinions range from absolute belief in to outright rejection of UFOs. This spectrum of believers breaks down into the following broad categories:

UFO Buff (aka True Believer)

One who is utterly convinced that aliens are visiting Earth. A UFO buff, or true believer, accepts virtually *any* sighting or alien contact story as genuine. He or she tends not to look at evidence impartially and often ridicules people who think UFOs don't exist. Some UFO buffs consider themselves to be UFO investigators/researchers.

UFO Investigator/Researcher (aka Ufologist [yoo-FAHL-uh-jist])

One who accepts the possibility that alien entities are responsible for some sightings. A ufologist insists on rigorous investigation and documented evidence before drawing a conclusion about an incident. He or she is not necessarily convinced that UFOs are alien spaceships and often (but not necessarily) has a scientific background.

Skeptic (aka Open-Minded Skeptic)

One who is willing to keep an open mind on the subject of UFOs but is inclined toward disbelief. Skeptics are usually not is impressed by witness reports. They want to see physical evidence. Many skeptics do acknowledge, however, that not all UFO sightings have been successfully explained.

Debunker

One who is absolutely convinced that alien life forms are not visiting Earth. Debunkers believe that there are natural explanations for every UFO sighting. They often ridicule people who believe in UFOs and are accused by UFO buffs and some investigators of participating in cover-ups. Debunkers sometimes consider themselves to be open-minded skeptics.

Note: Throughout the book, you will occasionally see this icon. It represents a "Man in Black"—a mysterious figure who occasionally appears in connection with UFO sightings (for more info on the Men in Black, see p. 36). This icon signifies an incident that is especially well documented or thought-provoking.

Part I
Early Encounters
(PREHISTORY–1947)

"This is not simply a case of a few tales relating encounters between…humans and strange creatures from the sky. This is an age-old and worldwide myth that has shaped our belief structures, our scientific expectations, and our view of ourselves." —Jacques Vallee, *Dimensions* (1988)

BEFORE HISTORY:
Alien Encounters of Myth and Legend
(20 Million BC–3500 BC)

Flying saucers. Alien abductions. Creatures from outer space.

Although these seem like thoroughly modern concepts, they're really older than recorded history. Most ancient cultures around the world have stories about beings coming down from the sky, landing on Earth, and communicating with the natives—sometimes even abducting or killing them! Of course, the ancients called these alien beings "gods," and today we refer to their stories as "myths."

Some scholars believe that these myths have more than a kernel of truth at their core. They believe that hidden inside these ancient tales are stories about people's first encounters with aliens.

The Case for Ancient Astronauts

The theory that ancient Earth was visited by alien astronauts was first proposed by ufologists in the 1950s.

According to this theory, aliens arrived on Earth several million years ago—long after the dinosaurs had become extinct but well before human beings had evolved—and established an advanced technological civilization here. As part of a breeding experiment, the aliens created human beings from apes. The aliens put the humans in charge of Earth and left the planet, with promises that they would someday return.

This theory suggests that the foundations of the ancient world's religions—the gods of Greece and Rome, for example, and the divine beings of India and Asia—are based on dim memories of early human beings' first encounters with aliens.

In the 1970s, a number of authors wrote books expanding on these ideas.

Swiss author Erich von Däniken (EH-rik von DAY-nuh-kin), in his 1970 bestseller *Chariots of the Gods*, argued that there is evidence all over the world that

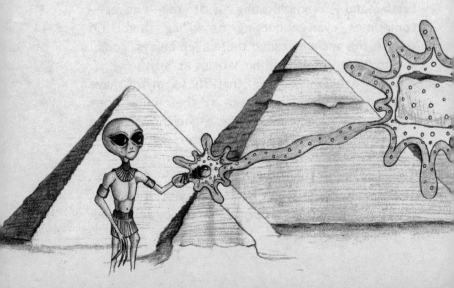

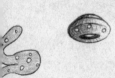 ANCIENT MYTHS	
WHERE	**ANCIENT ENCOUNTERS**
AMERICA (CALIFORNIA)	The Paiute (PY-oot) Indians have an ancient legend that people from space, called the *Hav-Masuvs*, traveled to Earth in silver "canoes." Their weapon was a small tube, held in the hand like a modern flashlight. "Rays" that beamed from the tubes paralyzed victims.
EGYPT	The god Horus appeared as a glowing flying disk.
INDIA	Beings who lived in the sky had a vehicle that could travel to the stars.
MIDDLE EAST (LEBANON)	The ancient Phoenicians (fih-NEE-shuns) wore amulets to protect themselves from flying disks that fired lightning bolts.
MIDDLE EAST (IRAQ)	The ancient Sumerians believed amphibious creatures from a distant star came to Earth and taught early human beings math, science, and the arts.

ancient astronauts visited Earth. His most impressive example: the pyramids of Egypt. These massive pyramids are built from tens of thousands of stone blocks, each block weighing hundreds of tons. Von Däniken theorized that human beings could not possibly have lifted such heavy stones into place, and that the pyramids could only have been made with the help of alien technology.

Zecharia Sitchin (zek-uh-RY-uh SIH-chin) is another writer with theories about ancient astronauts, which he outlined in *The Twelfth Planet*, his 1976 book. Sitchin is an authority on the Sumerian culture, which flourished on the Persian Gulf six thousand years ago. He taught himself to read its ancient texts—written in cuneiform (kyoo-NEE-uh-form), triangular characters pressed into clay tablets—and became convinced that the myths told the true story of godlike aliens visiting Earth. The "twelfth planet" in the book's title refers to the planet Marduk (mar-DOOK), home, Sitchin believes, of these godlike beings. According to Sitchin, the Sumerians predicted that the aliens will return to Earth in the year 2013.

The Skeptics Speak: Chariots on Fire

Most anthropologists (people who study the origins of humanity) and archaeologists (experts in ancient civilizations) consider theories about ancient astronauts pure nonsense. They say that von Däniken, Sitchin, and others like them misinterpret facts, twist evidence, and invent information. For instance, most Sumerian scholars today flatly dismiss Sitchin's interpretation of that culture's beliefs.

As for von Däniken, the historical record is clear that the ancient Egyptians built the pyramids themselves. They had begun generations earlier by making simple burial mounds. These became more and more elaborate as time went on, resulting in the gigantic pyramids we are familiar with today. The Egyptians also kept written records as the pyramids were being built—and these records don't mention any aliens. The other examples cited in von Däniken's book fall apart under similar scrutiny.

HISTORIC SIGHTINGS

YEAR	PLACE	THE RECORDS RELATE	WITNESS(ES)
1500 BC	EGYPT	Huge disks brighter than the sun race through the sky.	The pharaoh and his soldiers
322 BC	TYRE	Several flying "shields" circle over the city.	Alexander the Great's army
218 BC	ROME	A fleet of shining ships in the sky.	Hannibal's army
70 AD	JERUSALEM	Thousands of silver "chariots" racing through the clouds.	The historian Josephus
235 AD	CHINA	A red "meteor" circles an army camp.	General Chuko Liang and his troops
776 AD	GERMANY	Two red disks fly over a raging battle. One army flees in terror.	German and French soldiers
1211 AD	IRELAND	A flying ship's anchor gets stuck in a village church's steeple; a being from the ship tries to free it.	Churchgoers
1361 AD	WESTERN JAPAN	A drum-shaped object flies from the sea.	Villagers
1566 AD	SWITZERLAND	Battle between black and red spheres in the sky.	People of Basel, Switzerland

HISTORIC ENCOUNTERS
(3500 BC–1900 AD)

Writing was invented by the Sumerians around the year 3500 BC. In the years that followed, scribes throughout Asia, Africa, and Europe began writing everything down—from laws to laundry lists, from the acts of kings to the latest gossip. And every so often they recorded sightings of unusual objects in the sky. Wandering lights, flying ships, and aerial battles were common entries in the earliest written histories.

Most of these sightings were of natural phenomena, such as comets and meteors. Some, however, defy conventional explanation.

Agobard and the "Cloudship"

One early encounter occurred during the ninth century, in the part of Europe that is now France. It is interesting because the written account is more detailed than most.

Agobard, the Archbishop of Lyons, had taken to collecting and setting down the local folktales of a world said to exist above the clouds. The people of Lyons called this world Magonia. Agobard, a learned man, knew that no such place existed. However, he took great delight in tales of the place and its inhabitants, the "Sylphs"—who sailed through the clouds in great silver ships. These "cloudships," the locals believed, created storms, and when they landed on Earth, the Sylphs would come out and steal crops and livestock.

One day, Agobard received word that four Sylphs had been captured. He rushed to the scene, where he found an angry mob. Three men and a woman were bound in chains.

Agobard demanded an explanation. Several eyewitnesses reported they had seen a cloudship land, and that the four Sylphs had jumped out. The towns-folk captured them and, after some debate, decided the Sylphs should be put to death.

Agobard turned to the four frightened prisoners and asked them their side of the story. They had been on a cloudship, they admitted. But they were not Sylphs. They were humans—residents of a nearby town who had been abducted and held

**STAR DATE:
SEPTEMBER 24, 1235—
THE FIRST "OFFICIAL" UFO
INVESTIGATION**

The first official UFO investigation took place in Japan over seven hundred years ago! One night, several soldiers huddling in a military encampment saw lights circling overhead. This light show continued for hours, until it was nearly dawn. General Yoritsume ordered a "full-scale investigation," and the soldiers were interviewed by military officials. Their report blamed the incident on natural causes: "It is only the wind making the stars sway."

prisoner on the cloudship. They insisted they were guilty of no crime but had simply escaped from the craft.

Agobard was a wise man. He believed that Magonia was an imaginary place. When confronted with direct eyewitness testimony that contradicted his opinion, he didn't hesitate. He refused to believe either side.

"Magonia does not exist," Agobard told the crowd. "Cloudships do not exist. Therefore, these people could not have jumped out of one. Release them at once."

The crowd rejoiced that Agobard had discerned the truth, and turned the prisoners free.

A drawing of the mysterious airship sighted over Sacramento in 1896, as seen in the *San Francisco Call*.

The Great Airship

From 1896 to 1897, a mysterious airborne craft was seen by thousands of people as it flew across the United States. To this day, "The Great Airship," as it came to be known, has never been fully explained. The first sighting of the airship occurred on the night of November 17, 1896, in Sacramento, California. Hundreds of people saw a huge dark shape floating across the sky, shining bright searchlights toward the ground. Witnesses said the airborne vessel steered around buildings and avoided nearby hills before flying away.

A few nights later, the flying ship was back. It flew over Sacramento several times, again shining bright lights toward the ground. Witnesses this time included the city's District Attorney and California's Secretary of State.

No one had ever seen a flying machine before. Airplanes had not yet been invented. It would be seven years before the Wright Brothers flew the first airplane at Kitty Hawk, North Carolina. And although some inventors in Europe were experimenting with dirigibles (dih-RIJ-uh-bulz)—rigid balloons filled with hot air that could be flown and steered—none had yet flown for more than a few hundred feet.

More sightings of the same or a similar craft occurred over California for the rest of the year, usually at night. On the few occasions the airship was seen during the day, it was described as approximately one hundred feet long, cigar-shaped, and made of silvery metal.

Early in 1897, reports began coming in that the Great Airship was heading east. In February, it was seen over Nebraska. By late March, it was spotted over Kansas. It flew over small towns and large cities. Newspapers reported that large crowds of people would gawk as it passed overhead. Sightings of the airship ended in May 1897.

Was the Airship a Flying Saucer?
The airship was virtually forgotten after the sightings stopped—until the 1950s, when UFO investigators discovered the old newspaper clippings. The ufologists noticed similarities between the airship reports of the 1890s and flying saucer

THE USUAL SUSPECTS: VENUS

The planet Venus is the culprit most often cited to explain UFO sightings. Even ufologists acknowledge that Venus is responsible for many UFOs. Venus is one of the brightest objects in the evening sky. It can hang close to the horizon, giving the impression that it is a small object only a few miles away. Tiny movements of your eye muscles can also create the illusion that the planet is moving. If you see a bright point of light near the horizon and it doesn't seem to move far from its original position, get out your star charts and check the location of Venus.

reports of the 1940s and 1950s (see p. 22): the airship could fly fast or slow, hover, circle, and land; it could change direction instantly at high speeds; and when it left an area, it could vanish from sight instantly.

Airship Occupants

During its cross-country flight, many people claimed they met the airship's occupants. In most of these reports, the pilots were described as ordinary-looking humans who often asked for supplies, such as oil, water, or tools.

One such encounter happened near Hot Springs, Arkansas. A sheriff and his deputy were on horseback, following the trail of a fugitive. It was raining, and they were drenched. Late in the day, the lawmen claimed they saw the airship land. Two men emerged from the vessel, one with a long dark beard. The airship's occupants offered to give the lawmen a ride.

"We can take you to where it's not raining," the bearded man volunteered.

"We prefer to get wet," said the sheriff as he and his deputy went quickly on their way.

The Skeptics Speak: Hot Air

The first debunkers spoke up a mere two days after the first Sacramento sighting. The San Francisco Chronicle called the airship "probably one of the greatest hoaxes...ever sprung." But the Chronicle provided no evidence that the airship was a hoax and offered no explanation for the sightings. Other skeptics claimed that witnesses had actually seen a bright star or the planet Venus. The <u>Kansas City Times</u>, however, responded that the airship couldn't have been Venus since the planet and the airship were both plainly seen by witnesses. The newspaper also noted that the airship moved rapidly through the sky. "Stars do not perform these feats," the article dryly pointed out. "Neither do planets."

EARLY TWENTIETH-CENTURY ENCOUNTERS

During the first half of the twentieth century, people around the world continued to report appearances of remarkable objects in the skies.

As interesting as these reports are, a number of incidents stand out from the rest.

"Miracle" at Fátima

On May 13, 1917, three children tending sheep in a pasture in Fátima, Portugal, saw a ball of light appear in the sky. Inside the light they saw a beautiful woman who told them she'd come from heaven. She asked the children to return on the thirteenth day of every month and promised them that in October, there would be a miracle that everyone in the town would witness.

The children agreed to do as she requested. On June 13, they returned to the pasture accompanied by fifty adults. Again the woman appeared, but only the children could see her. Everyone, however, heard a loud "boom" when the visit ended.

Word spread. One month later, when the children returned on July 13, nearly five thousand people came to see what would happen. Again, only the

OTHER EARLY TWENTIETH–CENTURY SIGHTINGS

DATE	PLACE	THE SIGHTING	WITNESSED BY
February 28, 1904	OFF THE EAST COAST OF KOREA	Three large red egg-shaped objects approached U.S. Navy ship.	U.S. naval officers
September 16, 1906	SOUTHERN INDIANAPOLIS	A cigar-shaped object flying over the city.	Hundreds of individuals
July 31, 1909	SOUTHERN NEW ZEALAND	An airship-shaped object flew over three towns.	At least ten people
December 24, 1909	BOSTON, MASSACHUSETTS	A long tube-shaped object flew over the city.	Thousands of individuals
Fall of 1912	ALAMEDA, CALIFORNIA	Three pale green disks flew through the afternoon sky.	Three fifteen-year-old boys
Summer of 1913	LANSING, MICHIGAN	A golden oval flew through the evening sky.	Eight-year-old boy
March 1, 1918	WACO, TEXAS	A 150-foot-long, flame-colored, cigar-shaped object flew overhead.	Soldiers at Rich Field
June 8, 1920	KANSAS AND MISSOURI	A large cylinder flew over two states.	Approximately two hundred individuals
August 5, 1926	MONGOLIA	A huge, shiny oval object speeding overhead.	Crew of mountain climbers
Summer of 1933	OAKLAND, CALIFORNIA	Seven or eight balls of light with flames shooting out the back.	Two Boy Scouts
August 29, 1942	COLUMBUS, MISSISSIPPI	Two enormous red balls dropped to treetop level, then shot away.	Two Army radio operators
February 1945	EL PASO, TEXAS	A thirty-foot-long dull gray metal tube flew below an Army aircraft.	Three Army officers
May 1946	LA GRANGE, FLORIDA	A football-shaped object flying directly overhead.	A Navy lieutenant and his family
July 1946, and later	SWEDEN	Hundreds of rockets seen flying overhead, dubbed "ghost rockets."	Thousands of witnesses

children saw the lady, but the others there claimed they saw a white cloud in the field and heard a buzzing or humming sound. And again there was the sound of an explosion when the visit was over. On August 13, eighteen thousand people crowded into the field—but the children weren't there. They had been put in jail by a city official who wanted to "end the nonsense." The witnesses in the field heard the familiar explosion and saw a flash of light, but no one saw the lady. The children were released a few days later, and on September 13, they were back in the pasture—along with more than thirty thousand people. This time the ball of light was seen by everyone. Two skeptics who had come to find out what was "really" happening were asked what they had seen. "A heavenly vehicle" was all they could answer.

On the 13th of October, seventy thousand people squeezed into the pasture. Many hoped to see a miracle. Others expected to see nothing at all. Which would it be? everyone wondered. What, if anything, would happen? They were not to be disappointed.

Clouds that had filled the sky suddenly parted, and the sun appeared—an odd, silvery, disk-shaped sun that began to spin rapidly, shooting colors in every direction. Suddenly, the disk stopped spinning and fell toward Earth. People were terrified. The sun was falling from the sky and life on Earth was about to end! But the disk stopped in midair, then flew back up into the sky.

The spectacle was witnessed by believers and nonbelievers, rich and poor, laborers and lawyers, politicians and priests. Thousands prayed and wept. Most were convinced it was a sign from God.

What happened at Fátima? Was it a miracle? Or was it, as many skeptics claim, a case of mass

✈ INCIDENT AT FÁTIMA: M I R A C L E   O R   U F O ?

MIRACLE AT FÁTIMA	TYPICAL UFO SIGHTINGS
Glowing disk "dancing" through sky	Glowing disk moving through sky
Multicolored lights	Multicolored lights
Humming or buzzing sound	Humming or buzzing sounds
Vision of beautiful woman	Aliens described as beautiful beings
Loud roar at end of visits	Loud roar as saucers depart
White ball of light in sky	Bright lights in sky

hysteria—a delusion shared by an emotional crowd?

Or was it a UFO sighting? Many ufologists who have investigated the incident believe the "dancing sun" seen at Fátima that day was really a flying saucer.

The Great Los Angeles Air Raid

No one in Los Angeles during the early hours of February 25, 1942, will ever forget the fear and anxiety they felt that morning. The cause: an incident dubbed "The Great Los Angeles Air Raid."

Only two months earlier, the U.S. naval base at Pearl Harbor in Hawaii had been attacked by Japanese forces. The U.S. had just begun fighting in World War II. People were afraid of another attack on U.S. soil. Tension was high. Anti-aircraft guns had been installed up and down the coast of California to defend the country from enemy invasion.

At about 2:30 on the morning of February 25, radar screens picked up an unidentified target speeding over the Pacific Ocean toward Los Angeles. Minutes later, the object arrived and began to hover over the city. It appeared to be a gigantic sphere glowing in the sky. Anti-aircraft guns fired at it—and also at smaller objects that suddenly appeared, flying around the large sphere. These smaller objects zigzagged back and forth, dancing around the exploding shells. Witnesses said the small objects appeared to be "playing tag" with each other. The ground shook for over an hour as gun crews in the Los Angeles area fired at the unidentified objects.

THE USUAL SUSPECTS: WEATHER BALLOONS

When the Air Force began investigating flying saucer reports, they dismissed many sightings with the explanation that the witnesses had merely seen a wayward weather balloon. Occasionally, this did turn out to be the actual cause of a sighting. Ufologists, however, have uncovered official memos revealing that the Air Force often used the weather balloon explanation when they had no idea what really caused a sighting.

But when the shooting stopped, no one knew what they had been firing at. Although the soldiers who manned the guns, and the officers who commanded them, were convinced they had been shooting at real targets, nothing was shot down. The targets had simply vanished. The official military explanation for the shooting? People had seen weather balloons, and wartime jitters caused a panic. Few who actually saw the objects ever believed this explanation.

"Foo Fighters"

Between 1941 and 1945, American servicemen fighting in Europe during World War II reported seeing strange, brightly glowing objects in the sky: small fireballs of various colors, large red spheres, long metal "cigars," and silvery disks. Fighter pilots watched as these objects skillfully maneuvered themselves beside their flying aircraft.

Soldiers on the ground and sailors on warships reported the objects flying in intricate patterns high above their positions. Military personnel dubbed the objects "Foo Fighters," after a phrase

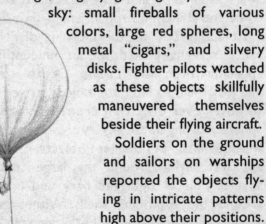

occasionally uttered by a popular cartoon character of the time.

Although the soldiers, sailors, and pilots mostly shrugged off the sightings, the War Department took their reports very seriously. Military officials were afraid the Foo Fighters were German or Japanese secret weapons. Military intelligence put a great deal of effort into finding out the origin of the objects—without success. After the war, it was discovered that German and Japanese troops had also reported seeing Foo Fighters—and that they believed the objects were *American* secret weapons!

The Skeptics Speak: Phooey!

After the war, the U.S. Eighth Army conducted a brief investigation into the mysterious Foo Fighters. Their conclusion: the objects were either natural phenomena or the result of mass hallucination. Case closed.

Part 2
The Age of Flying Saucers
(1947–1970)

"Maybe... the UFOs that have been reported are merely misidentified known objects.... Maybe the Earth is being visited by interplanetary spaceships. Only time will tell."
—Capt. Edward J. Ruppelt, U.S.A.F., *The Report on Unidentified Flying Objects* (1956)

THE PANIC MOUNTS (1947–1950)

In April 1947, scientists at the Weather Bureau Station in Richmond, Virginia, released a weather balloon into the sky—and were stunned to see it suddenly surrounded by several silver disks! Flat on the bottom and round on top, the disks were larger than the balloon and moving much faster. After a few moments, the silver disks flew out of sight.

A month later, a field engineer for RCA saw a similar object.

By the end of June, sixteen more sightings had occurred throughout the country.

The stage was set for a new era in alien encounters.

The First "Flying Saucers"

On June 24, 1947, Kenneth Arnold, a businessman who was also a deputy U.S. federal marshal, was flying his private plane from the state of Washington to Oregon. As he flew past Mount Rainier, a flash of light attracted his attention. He looked up and saw nine bright objects speeding across the sky.

He had never seen anything like them. Flat and nearly round, the nine silvery ovals moved in unison around the mountain peaks. They were traveling faster than any aircraft yet built. Arnold guessed he was witnessing a secret missile test.

After landing in Oregon, Arnold went to the local newspaper, hoping they would investigate his sighting. He described the objects he had seen, saying they "flew like a saucer would if you skipped it across the water."

The newspaper printed the story, and the reaction was immediate. At least twenty people called the paper to say that they had seen the same objects.

ALIEN EXPERT:
KENNETH ARNOLD

Kenneth Arnold was a respected salesman of firefighting equipment and a deputy federal marshal. After his flying saucer sighting over Mount Rainier in 1947, Arnold became very outspoken on the subject of UFOs. He appeared on television several times to discuss the mystery and was often quoted in newspaper accounts. He also helped investigate several sightings. Along with many other UFO investigators, he came to believe the saucers were alien spaceships visiting our world. In 1952, he co-wrote the book The Coming of the Saucers. That same year, Arnold had another UFO sighting near Susanville, California. He saw two objects, one of which was nearly transparent. As Arnold toured the country and spoke about flying saucers, the military and the media began to treat him with ridicule. Arnold eventually grew bitter and stopped speaking publicly about UFOs. A few years after he withdrew from the public eye, he had one more UFO sighting, but refused to report it. He wrote to a friend, "If I saw a ten-story building flying through the air, I wouldn't say a word about it!"

Newspapers across the country printed the story. One headline, borrowing a word from Arnold's description, called the objects "flying saucers." A new phrase had entered the English language.

The 1947 Flap

In the days after the Arnold sighting, hundreds of people reported seeing strange objects in the skies. This was the first flying saucer "flap," or cluster of sightings.

The flap began on July 4 in Portland, Oregon. Police officers, harbor patrolmen, and many other citizens saw five disks speeding overhead. One police officer described them as "chrome hubcaps" flying through the sky.

That night, the captain and co-pilot of United Airlines Flight 105 saw five disks flying past their plane at thirty thousand feet. A flight attendant was called into the cockpit and asked to look out the window. She shouted in alarm as she, too, saw the saucers.

Throughout the country, eighty-five saucer sightings were reported on that one day. And the sightings continued, nationwide, over the following days and weeks. For instance, on July 8, at Muroc Air Base in California (now Edwards Air Force Base), dozens of officers, airmen, and technicians saw silver disks flying through the sky. By the end of 1947, over 850 sightings had been reported across America.

The Skeptics Speak: Natural Phenomena

Throughout 1947, the Air Force received thousands of calls and letters from people concerned about the disks. Officials hoping to reassure the public provided three explanations for the 1947 sightings: people were seeing

STAR DATE: JULY 29, 1947— THE FIRST UFO HOAX

The first known hoax of the flying saucer era took place a month after Kenneth Arnold's sighting. On July 29, 1947, two Washington state harbor patrolmen, Fred L. Crisman and Harold Dahl, made the startling claim that they possessed fragments of a flying saucer! Their story was this: while boating near Maury Island, a few miles off the coast of Tacoma, Washington, they saw six doughnut-shaped flying objects in the sky. Dahl had a movie camera with him, and he shot footage of the saucers. One of the disks seemed to be in trouble, and pieces of metal fell from it as it flew overhead. Crisman had fished some fragments out of the water. The Air Force was contacted, and two officers, Lt. Frank M. Brown and Capt. William L. Davidson, arrived to interview Dahl and Crisman. When faced with the two Air Force men, Dahl realized their "joke" had gotten out of hand. There was no film, and the fragments were ordinary aluminum. He admitted they had made the whole thing up. He and Crisman weren't even harbor patrolmen! Lieutenant Brown and Captain Davidson boarded a plane to return to California. In a tragic accident, the airplane caught fire and crashed, killing the two investigators. But a new twist was added to UFO lore: rumors quickly spread that the Maury Island sighting was genuine, and that the two Air Force men had been murdered because of what they knew.

the sun reflecting off clouds, they were witnessing
particularly intense meteor showers, and/or they were
mistaking unusually flat hailstones for silver saucers.

But secret military documents discovered by ufologists
in the 1970s revealed that many high Air Force officials
didn't believe their own explanations. According to these
memos, the more convincing sightings—especially ones on
military bases such as Muroc Air Base—scared them.
Although publicly the Air Force insisted the sightings were
of natural phenomena, in truth they had no idea what the
saucers were. For all they knew, they could be spaceships
from another world!

The Crash at Roswell (1947)

Early on July 3, 1947, Mac Brazel—foreman of the
Foster Ranch near Roswell, New Mexico—was
making his morning rounds of the property. As his
horse carried him over the crest of a hill, Brazel was
surprised to find the field beyond the ridge covered
with wreckage. Something, it appeared, had crashed
to Earth.

Brazel collected bits of the scattered debris.
Some of it looked like aluminum foil, but it was
different from any foil he'd ever seen. It wouldn't
wrinkle or stay folded, and it couldn't be dented—
even with a sledgehammer! There were also thin
broken beams of a lightweight, flexible material.

Brazel went into town a few days later and
showed some pieces of the debris to the sheriff.
The lawman didn't know what to make of the
mysterious material, so he contacted the nearby Air
Force base Roswell Army Air Field.

Major Jessie Marcel was sent to the crash site to investigate. He and another officer loaded as much debris as would fit into their jeep and headed back to the base. But first Marcel stopped off at home to show his wife and eleven-year-old son, Jessie, Jr., what he'd found. Marcel's wife noticed that the broken beams had writing on them. Jessie, Jr. said the geometrical markings on the beams reminded him of hieroglyphics.

The next day, the Air Force base's press officer, Walter Haut, released news of the find to the media. Newspapers around the country and radio stations around the world picked up the story, reporting that the Air Force had recovered a "flying disk."

But within twenty-four hours, the Army issued a "correction." At a press conference, military officials announced that there had been a mistake. The only thing found on the ranch was a downed weather

balloon. Major Marcel posed for newspaper photographers holding up a battered balloon.

Newspapers published the correction, and the story of the crashed saucer was forgotten. But years later, Marcel would claim that the press conference was a fake, and that the weather balloon he posed with was not part of the debris he had found on the ranch. He said the wreckage scattered across the field looked "like nothing made on Earth."

The Cover-up

Most UFO investigators believe the press conference was the first step in the longest, most successful UFO cover-up in history. According to ufologists Kevin Randle and Donald Schmitt (authors of the book *The Truth About the UFO Crash at Roswell*), once the crash site was discovered, the Army immediately sealed it off. No one but military personnel was allowed to enter or leave. Ranch foreman Mac Brazel was questioned and virtually held prisoner at the air base for a week. He refused to discuss the incident for the rest of his life.

The military collected every bit of debris at the crash site. And according to the authors, that's where they made the most startling find of all: four dead alien beings, presumed to be the flight crew of the flying saucer.

Randle and Schmitt found evidence that a secret, unscheduled flight left Roswell Army Air Field late on the night of July 9. A sealed crate, accompanied by six military policemen, had been loaded onto the

ET TERM: HANGAR 18

According to some UFO investigators, the saucer wreckage and alien bodies were taken to Building 18-A, Area B, at Wright-Patterson Air Force Base. In UFO lore, this site became known as Hangar 18. The Air Force maintains that no such building ever existed.

In the mid-1960s, Senator Barry Goldwater of Arizona said he was receiving about "a hundred calls a year" from people who wanted to know what the Air Force was hiding in Hangar 18. Goldwater, a respected senator, a staunch supporter of the military, and one of the most powerful men in the government at the time, was intrigued. He asked his friend General Curtis LeMay, the Chief of Staff of the Air Force (its top-ranking officer), if he could look inside the hangar. According to Goldwater, LeMay got mad and yelled at him, "Not only can't you get into it, don't ever mention it to me again!"

airplane. The plane flew to Wright-Patterson Air Field in Dayton, Ohio. Many investigators are convinced that the crate contained the bodies of the dead aliens. At Wright-Patterson, investigators believe the alien bodies were dissected and the saucer wreckage analyzed.

The Investigation

By the mid-1970s, the crash at Roswell had largely been forgotten. Then ufologist Leonard Stringfield began researching rumors of UFO crashes. He found

PLACES TO VISIT: INTERNATIONAL UFO MUSEUM

If you visit Roswell, New Mexico, make sure you go to see the International UFO Museum and Research Center. The museum was opened in 1992 by Walter Haut—the same Air Force officer who, in 1947, released the news that the Army had captured a flying disk. The museum contains photographs, documents, and exhibits on the Roswell incident and other UFO sightings. But don't be scared by the dead alien on the hospital bed—it's only a model!

witnesses who swore they had seen alien bodies at Wright-Patterson. One witness claimed a building at the base held thirty of these bodies.

In 1978, UFO researcher Stanton Friedman interviewed Jessie Marcel, the long-retired U.S. Air Force major who'd been sent to investigate the Foster Ranch crash site. Marcel described all that he had seen—from the wreckage at the site to the bogus news conference he was forced to participate in. Over the following years, many other people spoke to UFO investigators about what they had seen at Roswell. These include:

- Bill Rickett, a counter-intelligence agent at Roswell Army Air Field, who insisted that he helped with the recovery of an alien spaceship at the Foster Ranch in 1947.

- Brigadier General Arthur Exon, who was a lieutenant colonel at the Wright-Patterson Air Field in 1947 when the secret flight from Roswell arrived. In 1964, Exon became the commanding officer at Wright-Patterson— but he was still not allowed into the building where the wreckage was purportedly stored. Exon told investigators that a secret group of officers controlled the saucer evidence.

- Several Roswell residents who claimed they saw the bodies of the dead aliens that were picked up at the crash site. They hadn't spoken earlier because, they maintained, the Army had warned them to remain silent.

The Air Force Explains It for You

In 1993, the Air Force (under pressure from Congressman Steven Schiff of New Mexico) began a new investigation into the crash at Roswell. A year later, they issued their findings: there had indeed been a cover-up in 1947. But its purpose was to protect a U.S. spy mission, not to keep a flying saucer crash from the public. A balloon had crashed on the Foster Ranch—although not a weather balloon, as had been announced at the 1947 press conference. Rather, it was a spy balloon, part of a top-secret military operation called Project Mogul. Giant balloons were being used to carry electronic equipment high into the atmosphere in order to listen in on Soviet nuclear weapons' tests. One of these balloons, along with its electronic gear, had crashed. The secret flight, the fake press conference, and the rest of the cover-up occurred because the military wanted to keep Project Mogul under wraps.

Most UFO researchers, however, don't believe this explanation. There are too many inconsistencies, they argue. One example: a crashed balloon would not produce several truckloads of debris spread over nearly a mile, as eyewitnesses had described the Foster Ranch crash site.

So what crashed near Roswell in July of 1947? In spite of attempts by investigators on both sides of the question, there is no definitive answer.

THE CONTACTEES

From 1947 to 1951, approximately two hundred flying saucer sightings were reported to the Air Force each year. The witnesses were people from all walks of life who thought they saw something extraordinary, reported it to the proper authorities, then returned to their normal lives.

But in 1952, a different type of flying saucer witness appeared. These witnesses made wild and extravagant claims that went far beyond mere sightings. They claimed that they had been personally contacted by aliens; that they had been taken for rides in flying saucers, introduced to alien leaders, and given messages to relay to all humanity. This group of witnesses became known as the contactees.

George Adamski and the Man from Venus

The first contactee was George Adamski. He tended counter at a tiny coffee shop on Mount Palomar in California, a few miles down the road from the renowned observatory at the top of the mountain. In the mid-1940s, Adamski built his own makeshift observatory next to the coffee shop. When he told people that he ran an observatory on Mount Palomar, he let them believe he was referring to the famous one. In 1947, when Kenneth Arnold's flying saucer sighting was widely reported, Adamski claimed that he, too, had often seen saucers flying over his observatory.

In 1952, Adamski was driving through the desert with some friends when, as he told the story, he saw a huge saucer fly overhead. "That ship has come looking for me," he told his friends. Adamski stopped the car and walked into the desert. He returned to the car a little while later with a remarkable tale.

Adamski told his friends a small "scout ship" had landed and an alien had come out. Adamski described the alien being as looking human—tall, very handsome, with shoulder-length blond hair and piercing blue eyes. The alien communicated with Adamski using sign language, simple words, and "mind-reading."

ALIEN EXPERTS: JIM AND CORAL LORENZEN

Jim and Coral Lorenzen of Sturgeon Bay, Wisconsin, founded APRO (Aerial Phenomena Research Organization) in January 1952. Jim was a computer specialist and Coral was a secretary before they began their UFO work. APRO was one of the first organizations committed to treating the mystery of flying saucers with scientific scrutiny. APRO's goal was to discover the truth about the saucers—which, the Lorenzens believed, were vehicles from other planets. The Lorenzens published several books detailing the cases they studied. Even if they weren't able to crack the mystery themselves, Coral explained, they wanted to at least record sightings in detail for later scientists to study.

He told Adamski he was from Venus, and that Adamski had been chosen by the Venusians to bring a message of peace to the people of Earth—along with a warning to stop contaminating our planet with atomic radiation. The being also told Adamski that there were many aliens on Earth, living secretly among us.

Adamski claimed he had several more contacts with the Venusian, along with some Saturnians and Jupiterians. He produced several photographs he had taken of the alien spaceships and published two books about his experiences—*Flying Saucers Have Landed* (1953) and *Inside the Spaceships* (1955). By the mid-1950s, Adamski was world-famous. He toured the world, speaking before thousands of people in every city he visited.

The Skeptics Speak: Out of Contact

Skeptics had a field day refuting the contactees' claims. They were quick to point out that many of the stories were scientifically impossible. For instance, Adamski's humanoid alien supposedly came from Venus. Yet life as we understand it could not possibly survive on that planet due

MORE CONTACTEES

Adamski was the first contactee to go public in the 1950s, but not the last. The best known among the dozens who followed in his footsteps were:

CONTACTEE	DATE OF CONTACT	HIS CLAIM	BOOK
DANIEL FRY, an engineer at the White Sands Proving Grounds, a military base in New Mexico	JULY 4, 1950	While everyone was away for the holiday weekend, Fry saw a flying saucer land on the base. When he reached out to touch the ship, a voice called out to him, "Better not touch the hull, pal. It's still hot!" The voice introduced itself as "A-lan." A-lan offered Fry a ride in the saucer—which sped him to New York City and back.	*The White Sands Incident* (1954)
ORFEO ANGELUCCI, an aircraft mechanic in Burbank, California	MAY 24, 1952	Angelucci saw a flying saucer hovering over a field. He approached, and a voice called out, "Don't be afraid, Orfeo. We are friends!" Angelucci continued to have sightings of the saucer, and after a few weeks the voice invited him aboard.	*The Secret of the Saucers* (1955)
TRUMAN BETHURUM, an operator of heavy equipment in Nevada	JULY 1952	While sleeping in the desert, Bethurum was awakened by a group of small men who took him to their flying saucer. There he met their commander, a beautiful female alien named Aura Rhanes. She told him she'd come from a planet called Clarion, which is always on the opposite side of the sun from the Earth.	*Aboard a Flying Saucer* (1954)

to its crushing pressure, toxic atmosphere, and extreme temperatures.

Most serious UFO investigators agreed that the wild tales of the contactees were no more than absurd fantasies. Two investigators in particular, Jim and Coral Lorenzen, co-founders of APRO (Aerial Phenomena

*Research Organization), were highly critical of Adamski
and the other contactees. The Lorenzens believed that only
serious scrutiny by the scientific community would solve the
mystery of the flying saucers. They feared that the
contactees, with their outlandish descriptions of beautiful
aliens and joy rides in flying saucers, would keep scientists
from seriously investigating UFO reports. Eventually, the
contactees began to fade in popularity, and by the late
1960s, they were little more than footnotes in UFO history.*

Albert Bender and the Men in Black (MIBs)

Albert Bender was a laborer at an assembly plant in
Bridgeport, Connecticut, who was fascinated with
the subject of flying saucers. In 1952, he founded the
IFSB (International Flying Saucer Bureau), an
organization dedicated to studying and—he
hoped—contacting the occupants of flying saucers.
In a few short months, his group had thousands of
members in countries around the world.

But less than a year later, a frightened Bender shut
down the group. He confided to friends that three
men wearing black suits had threatened to kill him if
he didn't stop investigating UFOs. At first Bender
suspected the men in black were government
agents, but he later came to believe they were aliens
disguised as human beings.

One of Bender's friends, Gray Barker, investigated
Bender's story. He found that many other UFO
investigators had also suddenly stopped their
activities—sometimes under mysterious circumstances. Were they, too, silenced by the Men in Black

(or MIBs)? Barker published his findings in a book, *They Knew Too Much About Flying Saucers* (1956).

Albert Bender wrote his own book about his experiences, *Flying Saucers and the Three Men* (1962). Many UFO investigators felt his description of his confrontation with the Men in Black read like a scene out of a bad science-fiction movie. The MIBs had suddenly materialized in Bender's bedroom, their eyes glowing brightly from within. They then took him for a ride to the Antarctic in their flying saucer and told him they were on Earth to collect seawater. The story Bender told was so outlandish that only a few UFO buffs believed it. Most UFO investigators dismissed him as another contactee.

But then something very odd began to happen. Ominous visits by men in dark suits began to be reported by other witnesses—people who had

never heard of Bender or his encounter. Whether Bender's experience was imagined or not, the Men in Black had taken on a life of their own.

A Visit by the Men in Black

Typically, MIBs arrive to confront a witness of a UFO sighting shortly after a sighting occurs—sometimes before the witness has told anyone about it. The visit usually takes place when the witness is alone.

MIBs tend to arrive in threes, usually in a black car—oftentimes a Cadillac. They wear black suits, which may appear ill-fitting and/or out of style, or dark military uniforms. They flash official-looking government IDs.

It is reported that MIBs display no expression on their faces, and their movements and gestures are

---

ALIEN FUN FACT: MIBS THROUGHOUT HISTORY

Folklorists point out that Men in Black, in one form or another, appear in the folklore of many countries. Almost always associated with demonic forces, they wore black robes, arrived on black horses, and usually traveled in threes.

The ancient traditions of China, India, and Tibet, for instance, mention an underground city whose inhabitants sent spies to the surface, usually in groups of three. These spies always dressed in black. Other ancient Eastern mystical sects believed in a group known as "Brothers of the Shadow," who silenced people who got too close to their secrets. Historian William Woods noted that the devil of folklore is usually described as dressed in black and "always in the fashion of the day." And folklorist Thomas Bullard adds that the devil is often said to ride in a black carriage—which parallels the black Cadillac of today's MIBs.

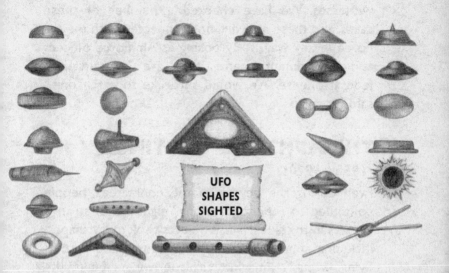

UFO
SHAPES
SIGHTED

awkward and stiff. Their voices sometimes sound unnatural or mechanical, and they are said to speak either broken or overly precise English. Encounters always end with a warning from the MIBs not to discuss them or the witness's original UFO sighting. Many people who claim to have encountered MIBs are convinced they are not human.

The Air Force on MIBs

The Air Force has known about the Men in Black since the mid-1960s. Col. George Freeman, a Pentagon spokesman for Project Blue Book (p. 76), admitted as much to UFO researcher John Keel in 1967. "Mysterious men dressed in Air Force uniforms or bearing impressive credentials from government agencies have been 'silencing' UFO witnesses. We have checked a number of these cases, and these men are not connected with the Air Force in any way.... By posing as Air Force officers and government agents, they are committing a federal offense. We would sure like to catch one," said Freeman.

THE SIGHTINGS CONTINUE
(1950s–1970s)

Even during the heyday of the contactees, people continued to report "ordinary" sightings of strange objects in the skies. These objects took many shapes, including: spheres with rotating lights, giant "cigars," flying "wings" (imagine airplane wings minus the airplane), floating cones, spinning spindles (two cones attached at their wide ends), and, of course, classic "flying saucers."

Most of these reports occurred with little publicity. Newspapers had long since stopped reporting most flying saucer sightings. But one high-profile sighting in Washington, D.C., was about to change that.

UFOs over the White House (1952)

For years, debunkers have asked, "If UFOs are real, why doesn't one land on the White House lawn?" Well, for a few hours in 1952, it seemed as if that was about to happen!

July 19, 1952, approximately 11:40 p.m. Radar screens at Washington National Airport in Alexandria, Virginia—just three miles south of Washington, D.C.—pick up eight unidentified blips. Operators watch as the blips travel over the airport and toward the White House and the Capitol Building—some of the most restricted airspace in the country. The supervisor at Washington National immediately alerts Andrews Air Force Base in Maryland, a few miles southeast of the nation's capital. The tower operators at Andrews have no idea what the objects are.

The blips pass over the White House and continue on toward Andrews Air Force Base. When one tower operator at Andrews looks up in the sky, he sees an enormous orange ball hovering above. The ball then suddenly takes off, moving at "unbelievable speed." Two fighter jets are sent after the lights, but the objects disappear as the jets approach.

THE USUAL SUSPECTS: TEMPERATURE INVERSIONS

Temperature inversions occur when a layer of warm air floats above a layer of cooler air. This is a temporary reversal of the normal state of the atmosphere, in which the temperature of the air is usually colder at higher altitudes. During an inversion, the surface where the layers of warm and cold air meet is known to reflect radar waves, creating phantom blips on radar screens.

One week later, on the night of July 26, the blips are back on the radar screens at Washington National Airport. Pilots of commercial jets flying into the area begin radioing in—they're seeing red-orange and white lights in the sky over Washington, D.C. People on the ground report seeing spinning lights of changing colors.

Air Force fighter jets are again ordered after the mystery objects. But this time the bright lights seem to play with the jets! Each time the fighters close in on the lights, the objects move away at tremendous speed, then stop and wait for the planes to catch up. Then, suddenly, the objects change the rules. They surround one of the jets. As the pilot nervously radios for help, the lights fly away and disappear from view.

The Air Force Responds

On July 29, 1952, the Air Force held their largest press conference since the end of World War II. The room was packed with reporters demanding answers. But Air Force officials laughed off questions about flying saucers. They explained that the blips on the radar screens were caused by an unusual, but perfectly natural, weather pattern called a "temperature inversion." The newsmen dutifully reported this explanation to the public.

But according to secret memos uncovered years later by UFO investigators, Air Force officials had no solid evidence that this was the

EARLY PHOTOS AND FILMS

For years people have come forward with photographs they claim to have taken of flying saucers. When analyzed, most of these photos have turned out to be fakes. But a handful of them, and films, have held up under the scrutiny of experts.

THE TRENT PHOTOS (1950)

Early in the evening of May 11, 1950, Mr. and Mrs. Paul Trent of McMinnville, Oregon, reported seeing a slow-moving object hovering in the sky over their home. Mr. Trent ran into the house and grabbed a camera. He managed to take two snapshots of the thing before it flew from view. The photographs show a solid, disk-shaped object flying near their house.

The pictures were published in the June 26, 1950, issue of Life magazine. Skeptics have claimed that the object is a small model hanging on a string. But the negatives have been subjected to exhaustive examination, including computer analysis in the late 1980s. No trace of a string could be found, and the object itself was estimated to be up to one hundred feet in diameter.

THE MARIANA FILM (1950)

On the morning of August 15, 1950, Nicholas Mariana, general manager of a baseball team in Great Falls, Montana, was checking out the stadium in town. When he went up into the bleachers, he saw two disk-shaped objects flying above him. He ran for his movie camera, which he had brought to the stadium, and aimed it at the sky, capturing two bright dots of light on film.

Mariana turned the film over to the Air Force for analysis. After extensive study, the Air Force determined that the lights were not reflections from birds, planes, or balloons. They could only be classified as unknowns.

THE NEWHOUSE FILM (1952)

At nearly noon on July 2, 1952, Navy Commander Delbert C. Newhouse was driving outside Tremonton, Utah, when he saw twelve disks flying through the sky.

Newhouse quickly stopped his car, ran around to his trunk, and got out his movie camera. But by the time he had the camera running, the objects were little more than specks of light in the sky. Still, Newhouse got seventy-five seconds' worth of the dancing lights on film before they disappeared altogether.

Newhouse gave the film to the Navy Photo Interpretation Lab, which spent nearly one thousand hours analyzing it without being able to identify the lights. They were convinced that the objects were not birds, airplanes, or rockets of any kind. The objects remain classified as unknowns.

One of the famous "McMinnville photos" taken by Paul Trent.

A blowup of the McMinnville UFO.

true explanation. Furthermore, the radar operators on duty during the sightings—none of whom was allowed to speak at the press conference—were familiar with the ghostly blips caused by temperature inversions. The operators were convinced that the targets they were following in July 1952 were not an inversion, but solid objects.

National Flying Saucer Flaps

After the first great nationwide flying saucer flap in 1947 (p. 24), several mini-flaps occurred over various regions of the country. These mini-flaps continued to take place regularly, and still do so today. But there have been only four great national flaps, when reports of flying saucers poured in from across the country simultaneously—from San Diego, California, to Bangor, Maine, from Seattle, Washington, to Miami, Florida.

The 1952 Flap

The "Great Flap" of 1952 began in June. By the end of the year, there had been over fifteen hundred sightings throughout the country. The Air Force identified most of these as ordinary objects (such as the planet Venus, weather balloons, or satellites) and unusual weather conditions. Nearly three hundred detailed sightings, however, remained unexplained.

One of the most puzzling sightings of the 1952 flap occurred on July 14 at 8:12 p.m., high over Chesapeake Bay. William Nash, the pilot of a commercial airliner, and his co-pilot, William Fortenberry, saw six flat, round disks, glowing a brilliant orange-red, flying directly toward them. The disks, moving together in a straight line, suddenly flipped onto their sides, changed direction, and sped away from the plane, disappearing in the distance. The entire sighting lasted less than fifteen seconds.

What had they seen? Debunker Donald Menzel (p. 78) dismissed the sighting as a red searchlight shining on clouds. Nash and Fortenberry said that was impossible—they had seen searchlights on clouds before, and that was simply not what they saw. Menzel's explanation was further weakened when weather records were checked, and it was discovered that there were no clouds over Chesapeake Bay that night.

The 1957 Flap

The 1957 flap began with a sighting on the night of November 2, 1957. Two farm workers, driving a pickup outside of Levelland, Texas, looked up into the sky and saw a two-hundred-foot-long rocket shooting yellow flames, streaking straight at them. The truck's engine stalled and the headlights died. The men dove from the vehicle as the thing roared past overhead. Shaken, they jumped back into the truck, which started right up, and sped to the nearest phone to call the police.

Before the night was out, the same object was seen by twelve people in and around Levelland. All the witnesses in cars reported that their cars stalled and wouldn't start again until the thing flew away.

Although the number of UFO sightings had been rising in October 1957, after the Levelland incident sighting reports reached record levels. Over the next few days, the Air Force received hundreds of UFO reports from people all over the country. One that was taken very seriously came from the control tower personnel at Kirtland Air Force Base, outside Albuquerque, New Mexico. The military men reported seeing an egg-shaped, wingless craft dive toward the runway, stop a few feet above the surface, and hover for a few moments. The craft then climbed at an unbelievable rate of speed until it disappeared from sight.

Altogether, 361 UFO sightings were reported by the end of November. The total number of sightings for 1957 was over a thousand.

The 1965–1967 Flap
Late on the night of August 1, 1965, a mass UFO sighting occurred throughout Texas, Kansas, New Mexico, and Oklahoma. People saw diamond- and egg-shaped objects and multicolored lights flying at terrific speeds. Several radar stations reported that they were tracking unknown objects.

Over the next few days, people all across the country began reporting sightings. By the end of August, 262 sightings were reported (nearly ten times the previous monthly average), and the sightings continued at this rate for the next two and a half years! White and red lights over Maine; giant cigar-shaped objects over Massachusetts; globes with flashing lights over Rochester, New York; a yellow-green ball over Marin County in California; a white disk in Hawaii—these are just a handful of the objects reported during the flap.

The Last Great Flap (1973–1974)
Beginning in January of 1973, people throughout the country began flooding their local newspapers and police stations with reports of UFO sightings. Among the many witnesses were the governor of Ohio and his wife.

All the classic UFO shapes were seen: balls of light, silver disks, giant cigars, and even an object that resembled the Great Airship of the 1890s (p. 12).

Many of these sightings involved dozens of witnesses. In one incident, deputy sheriffs transporting prisoners in Texas saw a disk-shaped object over their vehicle. The disk, which had a red light on top and a yellow light on the bottom, followed them for nearly twenty miles. The deputies called for backup, and several police cars arrived. All the officers—and prisoners—watched the object hover for half an hour before it zoomed away and vanished.

When the flap ended in June of 1974, thousands of UFO sightings had been reported.

CELEBRITY SIGHTINGS:
GORDON COOPER'S NEAR ENCOUNTER

Astronaut Gordon Cooper never saw a UFO while in orbit. However, a remarkable event did occur in 1957 while he was an Air Force test pilot in the Mojave Desert. Three Air Force cameramen came to his room with an astounding story: as they were setting up to film a test flight, they caught a UFO landing on film.

The cameramen showed the footage to the skeptical Cooper. His doubt turned to astonishment as he watched a disk-shaped craft hover above the ground and land on a dry lake bed. After a few moments, the craft took off at a sharp angle and climbed out of sight.

Cooper called his superiors and explained what he had seen. A courier soon arrived and took the film away. Cooper has never seen it since, and the Air Force denies that it ever had such a film in its possession.

SIGHTINGS BY ASTRONAUTS

Some skeptics argue that if UFOs were real, they would be seen by astronauts. In fact, the following astronauts have reported seeing unidentified objects in space.

DATE AND VEHICLE	ASTRONAUT WITNESS	SIGHTING	COMMENT
April 30, 1962 *X-15 test flight*	NASA PILOT JOE WALKER	Photographed six cylinder- and disk-shaped objects.	*"I don't feel like speculating about them."*
July 17, 1962 *X-15 test flight*	MAJOR ROBERT WHITE	Gray UFO thirty feet from cockpit.	*"There are things out there! There absolutely is!"*
June 3, 1965 *Gemini 4*	JAMES McDIVITT	Photographed unidentified cylinder while in orbit.	*"They are there without a doubt, but what they are is anybody's guess."*
July 18, 1966 *Gemini 10*	JOHN YOUNG and MICHAEL COLLINS	Large cylinder and two small, bright objects.	*"Odds are the UFOs exist."*
December 21, 1968 *Apollo 8*	JAMES LOVELL and FRANK BORMAN	UFO seen near capsule.	*"We have a bogey at ten o'clock high!"*
July 19, 1969 *Apollo 11*	NEIL ARMSTRONG and MICHAEL COLLINS	Photographed glowing object near the moon.	*"It was really weird."*

UFO Sightings Around the World

Flying saucer sightings in modern times have not been confined to the United States. From the 1940s on, flying saucers were reported all over the globe. One of the best documented international sightings occurred on September 19, 1952, in Yorkshire, England. A military airplane was coming in for a landing when personnel aboard the plane and on the ground saw that the aircraft was being followed by a silver disk. The disk slowed; then, as one witness reported, "It seemed to remain suspended in the air, revolving like a top." Then the object shot away and disappeared, remaining unexplained.

Other countries also experienced waves of sightings. For instance, France and South America both experienced UFO flaps in 1954. The French wave included two hundred UFO landings. Many of the UFOs were seen by several witnesses at once—in one case, approximately a hundred people in one town saw several crescent-shaped UFOs dancing in the sky for nearly half an hour.

ALIEN ENCOUNTERS — THE FIRST "OCCUPANT REPORTS"

During the 1950s, ufologists also became aware of a number of puzzling UFO reports from people claiming to have encountered occupants of flying saucers. These "occupant reports" were at first dismissed by serious ufologists, who thought the stories sounded too much like the tall tales of the contactees (p. 32). Most ufologists believed the contactees were making a mockery of the UFO mystery and didn't want anything to do with them. But one ufologist, Isabel Davis, investigated several of these occupant reports and came to the conclusion that the people reporting these incidents made very different claims than the contactees (see chart below).

After weighing the evidence, ufologists eventually concluded that some people had actually had that rarest, and scariest, of all alien encounters—a face-to-face meeting.

Sampler of Alien Encounters
Italian Alps (1947)
The first reported direct alien encounter of the flying saucer era occurred on the morning of August 14, 1947. Rapuzzi Johannis, a geologist hiking in the Italian Alps, saw two boys standing near a metal disk some distance ahead. According to Johannis, as he got nearer he realized the boys weren't boys, but instead were small humanoid creatures with

CONTACTEES VS. OCCUPANTS

Isabel Davis was among the first serious ufologists to dismiss the claims of the contactees, whom she believed were greedy opportunists. On the other hand, she felt that many occupant reports sounded believable, and the witnesses genuine. The difference, she felt, was in the simple, credible details of the occupant witnesses, as opposed to the exaggerated, grandiose claims of the contactees.

THE CONTACTEES	OCCUPANT REPORTS
ALIENS ARE TALL, BEAUTIFUL, HUMAN-LIKE.	Aliens look nothing like humans.
ALIENS ARE LOVING, FRIENDLY.	Aliens either ignore the witness or are unfriendly.
ALIENS UTTER LOFTY MESSAGES OF PEACE AND LOVE.	Aliens do not communicate at all or speak in a language the witness does not understand.
CONTACTEE FEELS "CHOSEN," IS PLEASED BY CONTACT WITH ALIENS.	Witness is frightened and baffled by the experience.
CONTACTEE WANTS TO SEE ALIEN AGAIN.	Witness wishes sighting never took place.
CONTACTEE SEEKS FAME AFTER CONTACT WITH ALIEN.	Witness only wants to be left alone.
CONTACTEE GIVES LECTURES, WRITES BOOKS, MAKES MONEY FROM THE INCIDENT.	After witness makes report, just wants to forget about incident.

oversized, hairless heads, huge eyes, and gray skin. One creature touched his belt, and a ray of light hit Johannis, knocking him to the ground. He remained conscious, but was unable to move as the aliens returned to the disk—their ship—and lifted off.

Bloomington, California (1951)

In September 1951, five people in a Bloomington, California, trailer park saw a flying saucer hovering twenty feet above them. They saw four human-looking aliens peering out at them through windows in the sides of the craft. The aliens had shoulder-length blond hair and wore blue one-piece outfits. When one of the women on the ground shone a bright flashlight at the saucer, it sped away.

Flatwoods, West Virginia (1952)

Early in the evening on September 12, 1952, in Flatwoods, West Virginia, three boys playing football, a teenager out hiking, and a woman with three small children saw a red light cross the sky and drop behind a nearby hill. Thinking a meteorite had landed, the teen convinced everyone to go look for it.

Deep in the dark woods, they found a glowing red sphere the size of a small house. Suddenly, there was a flash of light and a movement to their right. The teenager turned his flashlight. An alien being stood there, measuring about six feet tall. It wore a helmet shaped like "an ace of spades." From behind a round window in the helmet, two blue lights gleamed. As the being began to glide toward the group, the teenager dropped his flashlight and fainted. The others grabbed the teen, dragged him out of the woods, and ran to the local police station.

The next morning, the editor of the local paper visited the scene. He found a flattened area where the huge red ball had been and "skid marks" where the creature had been standing. The press dubbed the being "The Flatwoods Monster."

ALIEN EXPERT:
ISABEL DAVIS

Isabel Davis became interested in UFOs soon after Kenneth Arnold's sighting. In 1954, she co-founded CSI (Civilian Saucer Intelligence), a UFO investigation group whose goal was to apply scientific principles to the investigation of flying saucers. While very critical of the contactee movement (p. 32), Davis was one of the first ufologists who argued in favor of taking "occupant reports" seriously. In 1966, she went to work for NICAP (National Investigations Committee on Aerial Phenomena), another science-based UFO organization, and remained active in that group until the mid-1970s.

Nouâtre, France (1954)

At 4:30 in the afternoon on November 30, 1954, eight workers at a construction site in Nouâtre, France, saw a brightly shining domed craft floating three feet in the air. A man wearing a metal helmet and a one-piece outfit stood near the floating craft. The foreman of the work crew walked toward the strange man, who aimed a short tube at him. All of the workers were immediately paralyzed. The strange man disappeared before their eyes, as if by magic. The ship then rose jerkily into the sky, until it too disappeared. The workers were frozen until the ship was gone from sight.

Kelly, Kentucky (1955)

On the night of August 21, 1955, eleven people in a farmhouse outside Kelly, Kentucky, had what might be the most frightening alien encounter on record. Early in the evening, one of the men—Billy Ray Taylor—went outside to fetch water from a well. Moments later, he rushed inside and announced that a flying saucer had landed in a nearby gully. No one believed him.

A little while later, according to the witnesses, a short glowing creature entered the front yard. It had a large head, pointed ears, long arms with claws in lieu of hands, and big glowing eyes. Two brothers who lived in the house, Taylor and Lucky Sutton, grabbed a shotgun and a rifle, stepped into the doorway, and fired at the creature. It fell over, but then used its long arms to push itself back up! The thing scooted around the side of the house. The

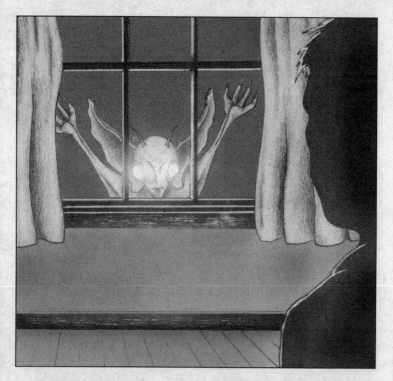

brothers ran inside and bolted the door. When
another creature looked in through the window,
they shot it, too. It fell, then flipped itself up and
scooted away.

For the next three hours, the men in the house
shot at the creatures (who periodically appeared in
the windows) while the women and children hid.
Finally, the occupants of the house were able to
make a mad dash to their cars and drove to the
police station, seven miles away. Local police, state
troopers, and military police from the local Army
base arrived at the farmhouse and searched the

area. They found many bullet holes and spent shells, but no trace of any aliens. At around two o'clock in the morning, the police and troopers gave up the search and left. The tired, confused witnesses went to bed.

Within minutes, however, the creatures were back. Throughout the rest of the night, the men shot at the aliens each time one showed itself. Finally, at nearly five in the morning, the "invasion" was over. The creatures were gone.

UFO investigator Isabel Davis (p. 53) met and personally interviewed the occupants of the house. In her report on the incident, Davis wrote that they seemed completely sincere, and she was convinced that something extraordinary had happened to them that night.

Dante, Tennessee (1957)

On November 6, 1957, a twelve-year-old boy in Dante, Tennessee, saw an object shaped like a giant egg in a field near his house. His dog was sniffing the thing. As the boy went closer to investigate, he saw

four human-looking beings standing outside the egg. One of the beings tried to grab the dog, but the animal backed away. The alien beings entered the egg—their spacecraft—and it lifted off.

Papua, New Guinea (1959)
On June 26, 1959, Father W. B. Gill and nearly forty other individuals at the Anglican Church in Papua, New Guinea, saw a disk-shaped UFO hovering in the sky. Four men on top of the disk seemed to be

THE "STAR MAP"

Much has been made of Betty Hill's "star map." Ten years after Betty drew it, Marjorie Fish, a teacher in Ohio, claimed she had identified the aliens' home world. Ms. Fish had built a model of a portion of our galaxy that accurately depicted the positions of forty-six nearby stars. She matched her model to Betty Hill's "star map" and concluded that the aliens' home planet orbited the star Zeta Reticuli. Many ufologists felt that a major riddle of the UFO mystery had been solved.

working on the craft. Gill and some of the other church members waved, and the men on the ship waved back. After half an hour, the object moved into a cloud and disappeared.

The next night it was back. Gill and the others assumed it was a military craft undergoing repairs. It wasn't until later that they realized they had witnessed something extraordinary. Thirty witnesses, including Gill, signed a statement describing what they had seen.

Adelaide, Australia (1964)

In 1964, in the city of Adelaide, Australia, seven-year-old David Mathlin saw a silvery disk land near his house. A human-looking creature with bright red skin exited the craft. The being, wearing black pants, a purple shirt, and silver boots, walked around the saucer, then climbed back into the ship. Although David was the only one who saw the alien, twenty people in the neighborhood saw the UFO lift off and shoot away.

The Skeptics Speak: Occupant Retorts

While most UFO investigators began to give serious consideration to occupant reports, skeptics and debunkers continued to scoff. They maintained that people who reported seeing occupants were hoaxers (or the victims of hoaxers), mistaken, or deluded. The witnesses in the Kelly case, for example, were ridiculed as "drunken hillbillies."

The Flatwoods case, skeptics determined, was a case of overactive imagination. The eight witnesses had seen a meteor fall. Then, while exploring in the woods, their flashlight had illuminated the eyes of an owl sitting on a tree branch, which they mistook for an alien.

The Hill Abduction (1961)

Early in the morning on September 19, 1961, an alien encounter occurred that was unlike any that had been previously reported.

Betty and Barney Hill were driving home from a vacation in Niagara Falls. After passing through Lancaster, New Hampshire, they noticed a bright light in the sky that seemed to be following them. Barney stopped the car and got out. The light came closer. It was a saucer, spinning in the air about eighty feet off the ground. Through binoculars, Barney could see beings in the windows of the saucer staring down at him. He jumped back in the car. He and Betty both heard a buzzing sound in their ears as they drove away.

A moment later, they heard the buzzing sound again. Alarmed, the Hills realized that they were suddenly several miles away from where they had been driving just seconds earlier. The Hills reached home without further incident, but later realized the trip had taken two hours longer than it should have.

Soon afterward, the Hills began suffering from nightmares. After a few months, the couple went to see a psychiatrist and, under hypnosis, they began to remember what had happened during

THE "STAR MAP": CONTINUED

Ufologist Jacques Vallee (p. 144) points to many problems with this conclusion, including one major flaw: Betty Hill did not draw her map to scale. There's no reason to believe that Marjorie Fish's accurate model corresponds in any way to Betty Hill's rough sketch.

the missing two hours. An incredible story unfolded.

After hearing the first buzzing sound, Barney had stopped the car. The UFO landed, and its occupants surrounded the car and opened the doors. They were little humanoid beings with gray skin, big black eyes, lipless mouths, and no noses—the first true "Grays" to be reported (p. 127). One alien pointed a small tube at the Hills, paralyzing them. They were then taken aboard the saucer. At this point, the Hills were separated and both underwent medical exams. Samples of their bodily fluids were collected. A needle was inserted into Betty Hill's navel. The aliens examining her said this was a pregnancy test. (A similar pregnancy test, called amniocentesis [am-nee-oh-sen-TEE-sis], is now a common medical procedure. But at the time of the Hill abduction, such a test had not yet been developed.) The aliens communicated with the Hills telepathically, and Betty was shown a "star map," which she later drew under hypnosis (see sidebar p. 58). The aliens pointed to one of the stars on the map, and Betty got the impression that this was where they came from.

The Hills' story was a terrifying departure from the simple flying saucer sightings and occupant reports that had come before it. The couple related many details about their encounter that would soon become classic elements of the growing alien abduction phenomenon: missing time, gray aliens, and frightening medical exams. John Fuller's book *The Interrupted Journey* (1966), which recounts their full story, became an instant bestseller.

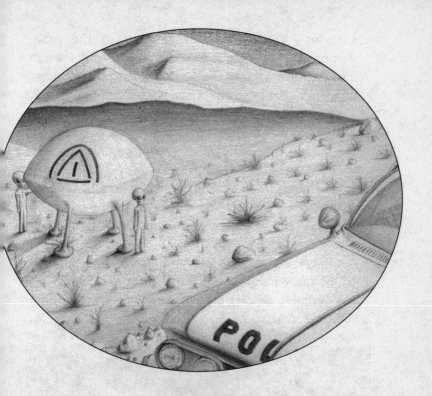

The Zamora Encounter (1964)

On April 24, 1964, a remarkable encounter took place outside the town of Socorro, New Mexico. It was unusual partly because of the credibility of the witness and partly because of the number of official investigators who tried to solve the case. In spite of their best efforts, it remains unexplained.

It started as a typical day for police officer Lonnie Zamora. Then in the afternoon, while pursuing a car down the highway, Zamora heard a loud roar in the sky. He looked up and saw a flame descending into a ravine—a wide, deep ditch next to the road. Zamora turned off the highway and carefully drove into the ravine. Near the bottom, he could see what he at first thought was a car that had flipped over, with two children standing nearby.

As he drove closer, Zamora saw that it was not a car, but an egg-shaped, silvery craft perched on four legs. And the two beings were not children, but small humanoid figures in white coveralls. One of them looked directly at Zamora, apparently startled by his arrival. Then the two beings quickly climbed into the silver egg.

Officer Zamora parked and was just getting out of his car when flames roared from the bottom of the craft. He quickly ducked behind his car. The ship

The depression in the ground allegedly left by the UFO witnessed by Officer Lonnie Zamora.

lifted out of the ravine, took off like a shot across the sky, and disappeared.

Zamora radioed headquarters, and within minutes his supervisor, Sergeant Sam Chavez, was on the scene. Chavez found a clearly frightened Zamora. The sergeant examined the site and found plants still burning and saw four imprints in the ground. Over the next few days, Air Force officials, FBI agents, and an Army captain from nearby White Sands Proving Ground (a top-secret military installation) investigated the case. They found that several people had called the police to report the loud roar, and a gas station attendant claimed a customer told him that he had seen the silver egg-shaped object cross the highway just before Zamora's encounter.

According to one official investigator, the Air Force was hoping to find flaws in Zamora's story, or to brand him an unreliable witness. They couldn't do either. Zamora, a longtime police officer, respected member of the community, and regular churchgoer, was interviewed for hours. All who spoke to Zamora were convinced of his sincerity.

Even the CIA (p. 77)— usually extremely skeptical of flying saucer reports—thought this case was different. In a secret report summarizing their investigation (found by reporter Howard Blum in the late 1980s), the CIA concluded: "There is no doubt that Lonnie Zamora saw an object which left quite an impression on him.... He is puzzled by what he saw, and frankly, so are we. This is the best-documented case on record, and still we have been unable, in spite of thorough investigation, to find the vehicle or other stimulus that scared Zamora to the point of panic."

The Skeptics Speak: The Zamora Hoax
Debunker Philip Klass (p. 146) investigated the Zamora case. He interviewed a married couple who lived near the gully. They were home at the time of the landing, with their windows wide open, yet they heard no roaring sound. Klass found other holes in Zamora's story: for instance, the object he claims he saw wasn't tracked on local radar, and nothing unusual was found in the soil samples. Finally, the condition of the landing site, with only a few charred shrubs, didn't jibe with Zamora's description of a large flame on the bottom of the craft, which Klass believes would have caused much more fire damage. Klass claims that these inconsistencies prove the Zamora case was a hoax.

Early Types of Aliens Encountered
Some ufologists are specialists in data analysis; they look for patterns that are hidden within mountains of data. When early ufologists began to catalog the hundreds of occupant reports they received during the early years of the flying saucer mystery, they found that the same types of aliens were being encountered over and over. The aliens encountered during this period of time could be placed into the following seven categories:

Hairy Dwarfs

Approximately three feet tall and covered with fur or hair, these creatures were humanoid in shape and walked on two legs. Hairy dwarfs were usually seen in groups of seven or eight, and they often tried to kidnap the humans they encountered. These aliens were among the most frequently reported throughout the world in the early days of the flying saucer era. No hairy dwarfs have been reported since 1954.

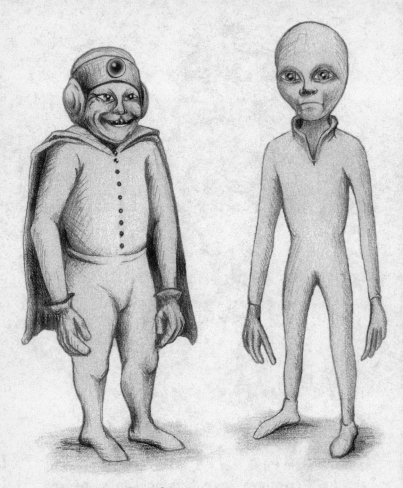

Human-like Dwarfs
Unlike the hairy dwarfs, these three-foot-tall aliens were more or less human in appearance. Although usually seen wearing militaristic uniforms, they were sometimes seen in slacks and shirts, and occasionally in metallic space suits. This type of alien is rarely encountered today.

Gray Dwarfs

Gray dwarfs were said to be about four feet tall, with gray skin and large eyes. Some witnesses described gray dwarfs as having deep wrinkles on their heads, while others reported that they had long noses. (These aliens appear similar to the Grays, aliens frequently encountered in abduction reports of the 1980s and 1990s [p. 127].)

Creatures in Space Suits

This category included any creature dressed in what seemed to be a space suit, with a helmet and breathing apparatus. Witnesses were often able to see the alien's face through a window in the helmet. Sometimes these aliens looked human, sometimes they didn't. Encounters with beings in space suits are still occasionally reported.

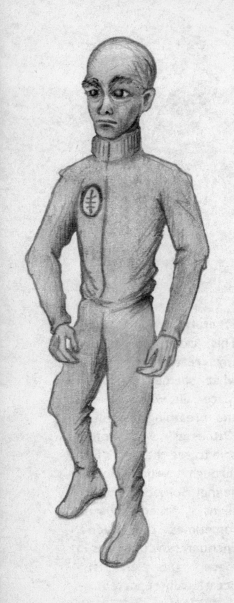

Ordinary Humans

These aliens resembled ordinary human beings. They were usually seen wearing coveralls or uniforms. Typically, a witness came upon one of these beings while it appeared to be repairing its spacecraft. The startled being would then hurry into its ship, which would lift off and fly away. Although this specific scenario is no longer reported, human-looking aliens are occasionally still seen in connection with alien abductions.

Beautiful Humans

These aliens looked like tall, blond, remarkably attractive human beings. The males were usually dressed in uniforms and the women in luminous clothing. Most ufologists regarded these reports with suspicion, as this was the type of alien most often reported by the contactees (p. 32).

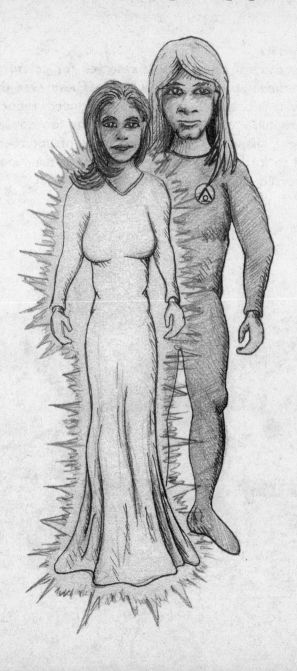

Monsters

This catchall category was reserved for creatures that didn't appear remotely human. These were the rarest encounters of all. They included reports of reptilian creatures, creatures that looked like octopi, shapeless masses like "sacks of potatoes," and so forth. These unique aliens were usually only reported once and never encountered again.

Part 3
The Official Response

"Flying saucers...exist only in the imaginations of the so-called witnesses."
—Report from ATIC (Air Technical Intelligence Center), 1955

OFFICIAL UFO INVESTIGATIONS

Over the years, the United States government has carried out many investigations into the UFO mystery. The Army, Air Force, FBI, CIA, and other government agencies have all studied the question of alien visitors. All these agencies insist they have never found any convincing proof that Earth is being visited by aliens.

ALIEN EXPERT: DR. J. ALLEN HYNEK

One of the most influential figures in ufology, Dr. J. Allen Hynek was hired by the Air Force's Project Sign as a consultant in 1948. Dr. Hynek had never intended to become a UFO expert. As head of Ohio State University's astronomy department, he was chosen simply because he was the closest astronomer to Sign's Ohio headquarters.

Hynek's original job for Project Sign was to be a debunker, providing ordinary astronomical explanations for the early sightings. But as the years went by, Hynek began reading reports that defied ordinary explanations—and he saw that these reports were routinely ignored or dismissed by the Air Force. Hynek came to believe that some UFOs might truly be extraterrestrial spacecraft. He urged the scientific community to hold a full, open-minded, scientific investigation of the phenomena. Such an investigation never occurred during his lifetime and has yet to be carried out.

Hynek's first book, <u>The UFO Experience: A Scientific Inquiry</u> (1972), detailed his years as a UFO investigator. It also introduced a new system of classifying UFO sightings.

Some critics, however, charge that these investigations were not sincere efforts to uncover the truth. Instead, say critics, they were cover-ups designed to keep the public from learning the truth about UFOs.

Have there been cover-ups? Or are government officials as mystified as the rest of us? What do they *really* know?

Early Investigations (1947–1952)

The Air Force took the first flying saucer report by Kenneth Arnold in 1947 (p. 22) very seriously. The objects Arnold reported were regarded as a possible threat to national security. As additional sightings were reported during the 1947 flap (p. 24), Air Force officials grew even more concerned. After analyzing the reports, Air Force Lt. General Nathan F. Twining concluded that the objects were real and were being controlled by intelligent entities.

Twining ordered the Air Force to begin a full-scale investigation into the flying disks. On January 22, 1948, the investigation began. Its code name: "Project Sign."

Project Sign (1948)

Project Sign was a top-secret investigation whose existence was known only to the most powerful men in the United States government. Even its name was classified and could not be revealed to the public. Air Force officials worried that if they gave any credibility at all to the UFO sightings, the nation would panic.

Project Sign personnel investigated 243 UFO sightings during the one year of its existence. All eyewitnesses were interviewed, and all sighting locations were visited and carefully mapped.

But within the first few months, the investigators involved in Project Sign divided into two opposing groups. The first group believed that alien spaceships might be causing some of the sightings. The second group felt that this view was ridiculous. These investigators were convinced that the witnesses were either mistaken, lying, or suffering from psychological problems.

THE HYNEK SYSTEM

Dr. Hynek's UFO classification system is still used today.

NAME	DESCRIPTION
NOCTURNAL LIGHT(S)	Unusual light seen in the nighttime sky, the most commonly reported UFO sighting.
DAYLIGHT DISK(S)	An unidentified object (usually disk-shaped) seen at a distance during the daylight hours.
RADAR/VISUAL	A UFO tracked on radar that is also seen by an eyewitness.
CLOSE ENCOUNTERS OF THE FIRST KIND (CE1 OR CE I)	An unidentified object, flying or on the ground, seen at close range.
CLOSE ENCOUNTERS OF THE SECOND KIND (CE2 OR CE II)	A close-range UFO sighting during which the environment is affected either permanently (through landing traces such as crushed grass) or temporarily (cars stalling, animals reacting, etc.).
CLOSE ENCOUNTERS OF THE THIRD KIND (CE3 OR CE III)	A close-range sighting of a UFO during which the witness also sees "animated entities."

The Air Force kept this disagreement secret. Publicly they scoffed at all saucer reports and issued periodic statements identifying all sightings as either outright hoaxes or simple misidentifications. In secret, however, the investigation continued.

The "Estimate of the Situation" (1948)
Near the end of 1948, members of Project Sign compiled the most plausible reports they had received from pilots, atmospheric scientists, and other trustworthy witnesses in a report entitled "Estimate of the Situation." The report concluded that these people had seen alien spaceships.

The Air Force chief of staff, General Hoyt S. Vandenberg, found this conclusion unacceptable. He rejected the report and ordered all copies of it burned.

Project Grudge (1949)
When the "Estimate" was rejected, the investigators who believed aliens were responsible for some UFO

ET TERM: UFO

The phrase "Unidentified Flying Objects" was used for the first time in December 1949, in the title of a Project Grudge report. This phrase and the initials UFO have since entered common usage. However, they are often used incorrectly to mean "alien spaceship." In fact, about 90–95% of UFOs do not remain UFOs for long. Upon investigation, most sightings turn out to be caused by man-made objects, astronomical bodies, or weather phenomena. (Less than 1% turn out to be hoaxes.) According to ufologist J. Allen Hynek, a true UFO is an object in the sky that not only puzzles the person who sees it, but remains unidentified after investigation.

sightings either resigned from or were forced out of Project Sign. Now the only people investigating flying saucers were the ones who didn't believe in them. Their job, as they saw it, was to convince the public that all UFO sightings had natural explanations. With this new mission in mind, the project's code name was changed to Project Grudge.

In 1949, Grudge received 244 new sighting reports. After cursory investigations, Grudge officials concluded that in each case witnesses saw ordinary objects such as stars, planets, or kites. Sightings Grudge couldn't provide answers for were classified as hoaxes.

As far as Project Grudge officials were concerned, the UFO mystery was solved. People who continued to believe in flying saucers were "nut-cases" or "fanatics." And although UFO reports continued to be received during 1950 and 1951 at the rate of about ten a month, Grudge stopped investigating them. Instead, they simply assigned to those cases the explanation they considered most likely.

The Fort Monmouth Sightings (1951)

A dramatic UFO flap at a military base in New Jersey changed the course of Project Grudge. On September 10, 1951, a radar operator at Fort Monmouth tracked an unidentified object speeding through the sky. Later that day, a pilot tried to intercept a silver disk he saw flying along the shore. The disk made a sharp turn and disappeared out to

ALIEN EXPERT:
EDWARD J. RUPPELT

Capt. Edward J. Ruppelt headed the Air Force's UFO investigation from 1951 to 1953 (from the end of Project Grudge through the beginning of Project Blue Book). While he remained skeptical of the extraterrestrial origin of UFOs, he was willing to keep an open mind.

In 1956, Ruppelt wrote The Report on Unidentified Flying Objects, a fascinating book detailing his years as the director of Project Blue Book. He was very critical of the way the Air Force handled the investigation of UFOs.

sea. The next day, several more UFOs were tracked on the base's radar.

Air Force officials hadn't been concerned about UFOs for years. As far as they knew, Project Grudge had satisfactorily explained all sightings as natural phenomena. These new sightings, by trained Air Force men at a military base, were a sudden, unwelcome wake-up call.

Top Air Force officials arranged a meeting with Project Grudge to hear the latest on the investigation. When they learned that Grudge was no longer actively investigating UFOs—that the project was basically dead—the officials couldn't believe their ears. They had been assured that all flying saucer reports were being investigated and that all sightings had been positively identified. "I've been lied to!" Major General C. P. Cabell, the head of Air Force Intelligence, sputtered with rage. He ordered the head of Grudge to begin a new investigation immediately.

Project Blue Book (1952–1969)
Hopeful Beginnings
In early October 1951, the head of Grudge retired from the Air Force, and on October 27, Air Force

Capt. Edward J. Ruppelt was named to head the project. Ruppelt was determined to lead a thorough, impartial UFO investigation. In March of 1952, Grudge's official name changed to the Aerial Phenomena Group—but it became better known by its code name: Project Blue Book.

Project Blue Book received almost 150 UFO reports that June—fifteen times the monthly average. In July, 536 reports came in (see 1952 Flap p. 45). While most of the sightings were quickly identified as ordinary objects, Blue Book considered the possibility that some could be extraterrestrial.

At the end of July, Ruppelt flew to Washington to brief the government's intelligence agencies (the CIA, Naval Intelligence, and Air Technical Intelligence Center) about the progress of their investigation. Many at the meeting were already considering the extraterrestrial theory, and Ruppelt was told to expand Blue Book's investigation.

Ruppelt returned to headquarters and laid out big plans. Blue Book was going to become the largest UFO investigation ever mounted. Or so Captain Ruppelt thought.

The CIA Intervenes
The CIA, or Central Intelligence Agency, is the federal agency that coordinates the U.S. government's intelligence activities. In other words, they are the country's top spy organization. The CIA gathers information on

ET TERM: FREEDOM OF INFORMATION ACT (FOIA)

The Freedom of Information Act—a federal law passed in 1966—allows U.S. citizens the right to request that the government release secret documents. If it is decided that the information requested will not damage national security, the document is released. Many UFO-related documents have not been released due to national-security concerns.

anything it deems threatening to the national security of the United States. At the height of the 1952 flying saucer flap, the CIA was taking UFO sightings very seriously.

One top-secret CIA memo from that period, released in the 1980s through the Freedom of Information Act (see sidebar p. 77), stated that the "alien origin" of UFOs could not be ruled out. It concluded that the CIA should continue to scrutinize UFO reports—and that the agency's interest should be kept secret.

A flurry of UFO sightings at Army bases and military installations throughout the country near the end of 1952 heightened the CIA's concern. The agency recommended that a panel of experts be established to evaluate UFO evidence.

The Robertson Panel (so named because it was chaired by Dr. H. P. Robertson, a CIA physicist) convened in January of 1953. Four other scientists were on the panel, including a colleague of Albert Einstein and a Nobel Prize winner.

ALIEN EXPERT: DONALD H. MENZEL

Throughout the 1950s and 1960s, Harvard University astronomer Donald H. Menzel was the nation's foremost debunker of UFOs. Menzel explained that all UFOs were caused by ordinary astronomical objects, man-made objects, or natural weather phenomena.

At the time, many scientists disagreed with Menzel's explanations, which they felt were often questionable and sometimes silly. J. Allen Hynek was his harshest critic, calling Menzel's theories "worthless."

Years later, it was discovered that Donald Menzel was secretly on the government's payroll. It is now generally believed by most UFO researchers that one of Menzel's special assignments was carrying out the Robertson Panel's recommendation to debunk UFOs.

But it was not to be the in-depth scientific study some investigators had hoped for. The Robertson Panel met for only three days and spent just twelve hours discussing a handful of sightings. The stacks of puzzling UFO reports from Project Blue Book's files were ignored. The Newhouse and Mariana UFO films (p. 43) were curtly dismissed. The Newhouse film—which the Navy Photo Interpretation Lab had spent nearly one thousand hours analyzing—was viewed just once by the Robertson Panel. The panelists decided that the bright objects in the film were merely reflections of sunlight on distant seagulls—an explanation Navy photoanalysts had specifically ruled out.

When the meeting was over, the Robertson Panel concluded that all UFOs were ordinary objects and that there was a reasonable explanation for every sighting. Furthermore, they found a "total lack of evidence" of alien intelligence at work.

Some observers felt that the entire conference had been a fraud. These critics believed the panelists had made up their minds long before the meeting began.

But the Robertson Panel wasn't satisfied with merely dismissing flying saucer reports. They recommended that the government begin a policy of actively debunking them. To this end, they suggested that newspaper and magazine articles be written providing commonplace explanations for puzzling sightings. And they

ALIEN FUN FACT: MOON DUST AND BLUE FLY
Even as they publicly insisted that UFOs did not exist, the Air Force was secretly developing two teams to deal with UFOs. According to a 1961 classified memo, Project Moon Dust would locate and recover alien ships that landed or crashed on Earth. Operation Blue Fly would then deliver the crafts to a secret location for analysis. But just as these programs were about to become operational, they were officially canceled. Some UFO researchers, however, claim that the projects were not canceled but were put into a state of readiness as planned.

directed Project Blue Book to stop investigating UFOs, instead ordering Blue Book to focus on supplying ordinary explanations for the reports it received.

Blue Book's open, impartial investigation into UFOs was over.

Blue Book Changes Direction

With the Robertson Panel's recommendations in hand, the Air Force transferred most of Project Blue Book's personnel to other assignments. Captain Ruppelt was left with just two assistants. In August of 1953, Ruppelt left the Air Force in disgust and returned to civilian life. With Ruppelt's departure, Blue Book stopped investigating UFOs. Instead, as the Robertson Panel had recommended, Blue Book personnel began to simply assign ordinary explanations to sighting reports.

Newspapers generally accepted Blue Book's findings and printed their explanations. But as sightings continued to occur, UFO investigators accused Blue Book of being little more than a "public-relations front." They denounced the Air Force for orchestrating a massive cover-up.

For years, investigators were convinced that when Project Blue Book stopped investigating UFOs, another military organization was secretly assigned that task. In fact, evidence of such a switch surfaced in the late 1980s: top-secret memos uncovered by UFO investigators hint that through the 1950s and beyond, a secret government group continued to seriously investigate UFOs.

The "Swamp Gas" Controversy

Project Blue Book managed to keep a lid on unwanted UFO publicity for fourteen years. Most of the American public believed that UFOs did not exist and that all sightings had natural explanations. That was about to change.

On the night of March 20, 1966, a farmer and his family in Dexter, Michigan, saw a brightly glowing object fly over their farm. Four similar objects were seen by many other witnesses in Dexter, including a number of police officers. The next night, in nearby Hillsdale, Michigan, nearly ninety witnesses saw another glowing object hovering over their town's small college.

Newspapers and TV stations around the country reported the story. People across the nation demanded an explanation from the Air Force.

Dr. Hynek, now a consultant for Project Blue Book, arrived on the scene in Michigan. He suggested that the witnesses had seen a natural phenomenon called "swamp gas" (see sidebar).

The eyewitnesses scoffed at this explanation. Newspaper and television reporters felt their intelligence was being insulted. The mood of the country suddenly seemed to shift. Congressman (and later, President) Gerald Ford demanded a full investigation. From 1952 to 1966, most newspapers had either ignored UFO sightings altogether or simply reported the Air Force's explanations. Now, almost overnight, Project Blue Book's credibility disappeared.

THE USUAL SUSPECTS: SWAMP GAS

For centuries, people have reported seeing strange lights in swamps. The lights have been given names such as "will-o'-the-wisp" or "St. Elmo's fire." We now know that these lights are natural phenomena. As plants die and rot, they produce a gas called methane. In swamps or marshy areas, this methane, or "swamp gas," will occasionally spontaneously ignite and burn itself up.

The Condon Committee (1966)

Uncomfortable with its new negative publicity, the Air Force wanted to dispose of the UFO mystery once and for all. They decided to hand over Blue Book's files to an independent scientific body for evaluation.

The University of Colorado accepted the challenge. Dr. Edward U. Condon, a respected physicist who during his career contributed to the

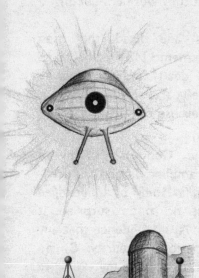

development of atomic weapons and radar, was named to lead the study.

Ufologists and others hoped for an open-minded, unbiased study. But the day after he was appointed committee chairman, Condon told a reporter that he had already made up his mind about flying saucers. He didn't believe in them. He said the purpose of his committee was to help people understand how they can be fooled by ordinary objects in the sky, and to study how mass hysteria begins.

UFO researchers were discouraged. Many believed the study was part of the ongoing cover-up. Others, more generously, thought Condon was about to bungle one of the most important scientific inquiries of the century.

Suspicions that the study was rigged were finally confirmed when a secret memo from the committee was leaked to the newspapers. The text of the memo revealed that the committee was really "a group of nonbelievers." "The trick," it read, would be to convince the public that they were conducting "a totally objective study."

Condon was furious and fired the men responsible for leaking the memo. He then began to fire everyone open to the idea that UFOs could be of alien origin. The three-year investigation then continued without any pretense of objectivity.

The Condon Report (1969)

In August of 1969, the Condon Committee published its report—a rambling, fifteen-hundred-page volume titled *Scientific Study of Unidentified Flying Objects*. To almost no one's surprise, it concluded that there was: A) no evidence that any UFO ever threatened national security; B) no evidence that UFOs represented any kind of advanced technology; and C) no evidence that UFOs were extraterrestrial vehicles.

In conclusion, the Condon Report recommended that the Air Force stop collecting what it considered to be useless information about UFOs.

While much of the scientific world publicly praised this conclusion, many thoughtful scientists were troubled by its inconsistency. To them it seemed Dr. Condon had not read his own report, for within its pages was the astonishing admission that some UFOs investigated may have been genuine extraterrestrial crafts. These included:

- A sighting at Lakenheath, England, in August 1965. The committee's investigator wrote, "This is the most puzzling and unusual case in the radar-visual files," as the "behavior of the UFO suggests a mechanical device of unknown origin." The investigator concluded that "the probability that at least one genuine UFO was involved appeared to be fairly high."
- Ten UFO sightings by astronauts, which the report said were "especially puzzling." The committee was able to positively identify only one of them as an ordinary object.
- The Trent photos (p. 43). After analyzing the original negatives, the investigator wrote that this was "one of the few UFO reports in which all factors investigated" indicate "that an extraordinary flying object, silvery, metallic, disk-shaped, flew within sight of two witnesses."

In fact, of the ninety-one detailed UFO sightings mentioned in the Condon Report, Condon's team was unable to identify thirty of them.

J. Allen Hynek was among those who criticized Condon's conclusions. Hynek pointed out that UFO sightings were being reported by thousands of people. To claim that such a widespread phenomenon was unworthy of scientific study—regardless of the cause—did nothing to advance science, argued Hynek.

PLACES TO VISIT: THE NATIONAL ARCHIVES

Project Blue Book's files are now located at the National Archives in Washington, D.C., where you are free to examine them for yourself. Their address: National Archives Building, 7th St. and Pennsylvania Ave. NW, Washington, D.C., 20408. Researchers under the age of sixteen must be accompanied by an adult. For more information, see the National Archives' Web site at www.nara.gov.

The respected American Institute of Aeronautics and Astronautics also rejected the Condon Report, stating that further scientific study of UFOs was required.

New York Congressman William F. Ryan went even further, attacking the report before his fellow Congressmen. "Public interest in UFOs cannot be wished away," he thundered. He correctly predicted that "reported sightings will persist."

There was one final odd note in the saga of the

Condon Committee. When the committee's work was done, Edward U. Condon had all of the committee's records—thousands of papers, reports, documents, transcripts of testimony, and handwritten notes—delivered to his home, where he burned them in his fireplace. To this day, no one knows why.

The End of Project Blue Book

The Condon Report signaled the end of Project Blue Book. On December 17, 1969, the Air Force announced that Blue Book was no longer necessary "on the grounds of national security or in the interest of science."

After twenty-two years, the Air Force publicly declared that UFOs were no longer their problem.

During its existence, Blue Book received 12,618 UFO reports. The Air Force attempted to assign an explanation to each, yet 701 cases remain officially "unidentified." (Ufologists who have studied the files place the actual number of unidentified Blue Book UFOs somewhere between four thousand and six thousand.)

Secret Investigations (1970s–Today)

According to government spokespersons, Project Blue Book was the last UFO investigation officially authorized by the United States government. But most ufologists disagree, claiming they have uncovered several top-secret UFO investigations since then.

UFOs over Our Nukes

In the fall of 1975, military personnel began reporting UFO sightings at air bases and missile silos throughout the United States. The first sighting occurred at Loring Air Force Base in Maine. A few days later, another UFO was seen over an air base in Great Falls, Montana. Minot, North Dakota, was next, and more sightings followed. The Combat Operations Center, the command center of America's air defenses, didn't know what to make of these reports.

After eight months, the sightings suddenly stopped. The Air Force was unable to identify the crafts that flew over their bases, nor could they determine how they disappeared without a trace at fantastic speeds.

According to official documents, top Air Force personnel were certain that these UFOs were actual crafts and not "misperceptions of ordinary objects or natural phenomena." At a secret briefing of the Joint Chiefs of Staff—the top military advisers to the President of the United States—Air Force officers argued that the objects were scout ships for a fleet of alien invaders. In the words of Howard Blum, the investigative reporter who uncovered this story in 1990, the Air Force began to secretly "prepare to do battle with extraterrestrials."

"Fast Walkers"

U.S. Department of Defense satellites have been orbiting the Earth for decades, monitoring the skies for enemy missiles. Data from these satellites is beamed to the ground every ten seconds and sent to the U.S. Space Command's Missile Warning Center, deep in the heart of Cheyenne Mountain, near Colorado Springs, Colorado.

Approximately two or three times a month, these defense satellites pick up UFOs—real objects that can't be matched to any known target—speeding through Earth's atmosphere. Defense Department officers have code-named these objects "Fast Walkers." The military doesn't know what to make of them and tends to ignore them.

ALIEN FUN FACT: THE NSA ON UFOS

In order to listen in on international communications, the National Security Agency has established electronic spy posts around the world. These installations contain the world's most powerful radio antennas and surveillance equipment. NSA agents staffing these posts have standing orders to alert headquarters immediately if they pick up signals or intelligent transmissions coming from outer space.

On May 4, 1984, an especially unusual Fast Walker was tracked for nine long minutes by U.S. satellites. It came from space, flew within a few hundred feet of a satellite, then headed back into space.

A full-scale investigation was launched, resulting in a three-hundred-page top-secret report. It was determined that the object was not a meteor, a man-made object, or any known natural phenomenon. It remains unidentified to this day.

The UFO Working Group

In his 1990 book *Out There*, investigative reporter Howard Blum revealed the existence of a top-secret government organization called the UFO Working Group. It was composed of high-level officers from the U.S. Air Force, Army, CIA, FBI, NSA (the National Security Agency—an intelligence agency even more secretive than the CIA), and other government agencies. The goal of the group was to use the vast military and scientific resources at their disposal to find a solution to the UFO mystery.

The group held their first meeting in Washington, D.C., in February 1987. Their first order of business: a thorough review of all previous official UFO investigations. They would then conduct investigations into select UFO sightings and aerial phenomena and monitor efforts by scientists involved in the search for extraterrestrial life (see SETI below). They also vowed to keep working as a group until they found an answer. In 1990, when Blum published his book, the group was purportedly hard at work. As far as anyone knows, they still are.

OFFICIAL ATTEMPTS TO CONTACT ALIENS

Although most scientists doubt that aliens are visiting Earth, many of those same scientists believe that intelligent life may nevertheless exist on other planets. Because the distances between stars are incomprehensibly vast and impossible to travel, these scientists reason, we must look for other ways to contact alien civilizations.

SETI (Search for Extraterrestrial Intelligence)

In 1959, Phillip Morrison, a physics professor at Cornell University, had an intriguing thought: what if civilizations on other planets use radio waves to communicate with each other? Radio signals, after all, are easy to transmit, easy to receive, and travel at the speed of light. Perhaps, Morrison thought, some worlds were beaming out signals in hope of discovering other civilizations!

On September 19, 1959, Morrison and another Cornell professor, Giuseppe Cocconi, published an article in the science journal *Nature* titled "Searching for Interstellar Communications." The article outlined their idea for SETI, the "Search for Extraterrestrial Intelligence." Morrison and Cocconi described how it might be possible to pick up intelligent signals from space using radio telescopes—powerful antennas designed to detect naturally occurring radio energy.

At about the same time, radio astronomer Frank Drake proposed the identical idea to his colleagues. Drake worked at an observatory in West Virginia. He believed their radio telescope could detect artificial signals from up to ten light-years away. (A light-year is the distance light can travel in one year. Ten light-years equals about 60 trillion miles.) Drake convinced his colleagues to begin hunting the galaxy for radio transmissions from other planets.

ALIEN EXPERT:
FRANK DRAKE

Frank Drake, one of the founding fathers of SETI, was only eight years old when he first wondered if life existed on other planets. Many years later, as a radio astronomer—a scientist who examines stars and other astronomical bodies using radio waves—he began trying to answer that question. In addition to his own efforts, Drake has encouraged other scientists to join the search. Drake is now the president of the SETI Institute (p. 98), based in Mountain View, California.

Early SETI (1960s)

On the evening of April 8, 1960, Frank Drake began our planet's first search for a signal from another world. Drake dubbed the effort Project Ozma, after the princess in L. Frank Baum's *Wizard of Oz*

THE ORDER OF THE DOLPHIN

In November 1961, Frank Drake invited a handful of scientists to a meeting to discuss how to proceed with the search for intelligent extraterrestrial life. One scientist at the meeting, John Lilly, spoke about dolphins. Dolphins talk to each other and have a complex culture, yet man cannot understand their language. If we can't communicate with an intelligent creature on our own planet, Lilly asked, what makes us think we could communicate with aliens? The group of scientists immediately dubbed themselves "The Order of the Dolphin" and resolved to consider this and other obstacles in the search for extraterrestrial life.

books. Drake pointed his radio telescope toward Tau Ceti, a star very like our sun. As the Earth rotated through the night, motors kept the huge antenna aimed at Tau Ceti. Tape recorders and computer printers were on and running. By morning, when Tau Ceti disappeared behind the horizon, no signal had been received.

The second night, Drake switched targets. He pointed the telescope at Epsilon Eridani, another star like our sun. Almost immediately, he picked up a signal: loud, clear pulses of energy at the rate of eight a second. After a few minutes, the signal disappeared. For the next two weeks, Drake kept the telescope aimed at Epsilon Eridani. For nine nights he heard nothing. On the tenth night he heard the signal again. Was it a

STAR DATE: 1972, 1973, 1977— GREETINGS FROM EARTH

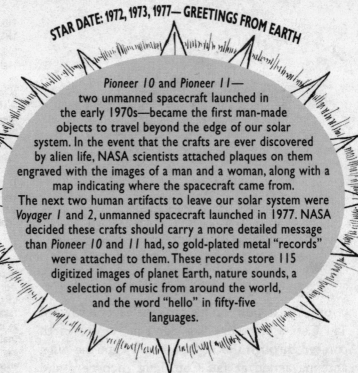

Pioneer 10 and *Pioneer 11*— two unmanned spacecraft launched in the early 1970s—became the first man-made objects to travel beyond the edge of our solar system. In the event that the crafts are ever discovered by alien life, NASA scientists attached plaques on them engraved with the images of a man and a woman, along with a map indicating where the spacecraft came from.

The next two human artifacts to leave our solar system were *Voyager 1* and 2, unmanned spacecraft launched in 1977. NASA decided these crafts should carry a more detailed message than *Pioneer 10* and *11* had, so gold-plated metal "records" were attached to them. These records store 115 digitized images of planet Earth, nature sounds, a selection of music from around the world, and the word "hello" in fifty-five languages.

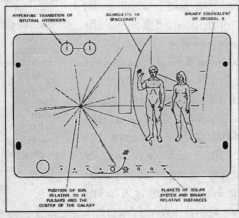

The plaque attached to *Pioneer 10* and *Pioneer 11*.

The gold-plated metal "record" attached to *Voyager 1* and *Voyager 2*.

message from another world, or man-made radio interference from our own planet? Frank Drake still isn't sure.

Project Ozma continued to target the stars for another two months, until the radio telescope had to be used for other projects. Drake never received another signal.

Drake's experiment intrigued many astronomers, but few had the time or resources to mount a search of their own. Then, in 1965, a team of Soviet astronomers stunned the world with the announcement that they had received a signal from an intelligent civilization. It turned out to be an exciting false alarm—the Soviets had actually discovered a new quasar, an astronomical object that transmits natural radio energy.

But the race was on. Who, astronomers wondered, would be the first to receive an intelligent radio transmission from another world?

The Modern Age of SETI (1970s–1993)

In the early 1970s, NASA (National Aeronautics and Space Administration), the United States's space agency, decided to pursue the search for extraterrestrial intelligence. Congress agreed to fund the project, and NASA

ALIEN EXPERT:
CARL SAGAN

Dr. Carl Sagan was the author of many popular nonfiction books on science and astronomy, but he may be best known as the author of the novel _Contact_, which was made into the 1997 film starring Jodie Foster.

Sagan was involved in NASA's _Mariner_, _Viking_, _Voyager_, and _Galileo_ expeditions. He also made important contributions to the study of planetary atmospheres, planetary surfaces, and exobiology—the study of extraterrestrial life. An asteroid was even named after him.

An avid supporter of SETI, Sagan was nevertheless an avowed UFO skeptic.

SETI@home

Scientists at the SETI Institute and the Phoenix Project receive more data than they can analyze themselves. To help with analysis, they are now trying to harness the untapped processing power of home computers throughout the country. This is how you can help.

At the SETI@home Web site (setiathome.ssl.berkeley.edu), you can download software for your computer that works like an ordinary screensaver, but does much more.

With the SETI@home software installed, your computer will be able to download a small chunk of the data that SETI Institute scientists have collected from their radio telescopes and posted on the Internet. Then, whenever your computer is turned on but not in use, the SETI@home screensaver will take over, searching the data for evidence of signals from another world. The results of your computer's analysis will be automatically sent back to SETI scientists. They will combine your information with results they've received from thousands of other SETI@home users.

began to develop SETI programs at its research centers throughout the country.

Harvard, Berkeley, and other universities around the country joined NASA in the search. Technologically, SETI became increasingly sophisticated. Supercomputers were used to filter out the noise of space and sort through millions of radio frequencies in seconds.

Unfortunately, after years of effort, no intelligent signals were received. One celebrated possible exception occurred at Ohio State University in 1977. A radio telescope wider than three football fields, nicknamed "Big Ear," was dedicated to the SETI project. One night in August, Big Ear picked up a steady, rhythmic signal coming from space. Then, as quickly as it began, the signal vanished. Luckily, the computer had been printing a copy of the transmission. A student volunteer, watching the machine, circled the wavy lines and wrote "Wow" in the margin. The incident has been nicknamed the "Wow Transmission." Whether this was a radio signal from a distant world or a stray man-made transmission is still unknown.

But disaster struck the SETI program in 1978. Convinced that SETI was a waste of taxpayers' money, Congress cut it from NASA's budget. Astronomer Carl Sagan met with the senators responsible for the funding. He asked them to imagine all we could learn from an advanced civilization if the search proved successful. Sagan managed to convince the senators that the potential benefits of SETI far outweighed the cost, and funding for SETI was restored—for a while.

To commemorate the five-hundredth anniversary of Columbus's journey to America, NASA was preparing in 1992 to embark on the most ambitious SETI program ever. Using the largest radio telescopes in the world and the most powerful receivers, NASA planned to target one thousand sunlike stars in search of intelligent signals. Simultaneously, NASA would use a network of radio telescopes to conduct a full-sky search, capable of detecting signals coming from any direction in the galaxy. It would be a ten-year quest to find alien radio signals. But in 1993, Congress again cut NASA's funding—this time for good. It seemed that the search for extraterrestrial intelligence was over.

roswell

ALIEN FUN FACT: NASA'S WARNING

NASA cautioned their SETI group not to reveal our presence to aliens. In an official NASA document, the space agency wrote, "To a very advanced race we might appear such a primitive life form as to represent delightful pets, interesting experimental animals, or a gourmet delicacy." But NASA's warning was in vain. Television signals have been transmitted for the past fifty years, and now extend fifty light-years into space in every direction. Any advanced alien civilization within that radius already knows plenty about us.

Beyond SETI (1990s)

Although government funding for SETI ended in 1993, several privately financed groups have continued the search. These groups include:

The SETI Institute

The SETI Institute, founded in 1993, is an organization of scientists and engineers dedicated to continuing the search for extraterrestrial intelligence. The head of the organization is Frank Drake. When NASA shut down its own SETI program, Drake arranged for it to loan its equipment to the SETI Institute.

The SETI Institute's first search, dubbed Project Phoenix, began in 1995. Its mission is to carry out NASA's planned ten-year search of one thousand nearby stars.

The Planetary Society

The Planetary Society was founded by Carl Sagan and other scientists in 1980, during the height of NASA's SETI program. Their objective then was simply to encourage space exploration and the search for extraterrestrial life. When NASA's SETI program ended, the Planetary Society expanded its mission. The group now helps finance SETI programs around the country.

One of the most ambitious programs began in October 1995, when the Planetary Society helped fund a SETI project at Harvard University. The project, called BETA (Billion Channel Extra-terrestrial Assay), searches for alien transmissions by combining ultrapowerful radio telescopes with supercomputers. The computers are capable of scanning a billion radio frequencies at a time, searching for intelligent transmissions.

The SETI League

The SETI League is a worldwide group of amateur and professional radio astronomers. The organization was founded in 1994, after Congress cut SETI from NASA's budget. The SETI League's most ambitious program is called Project Argus.

Argus was a figure in Greek mythology—a guard with one hundred eyes. Ever alert, Argus kept a few eyes open even while sleeping so no one could escape him. Project Argus plans to set up five thousand small but powerful radio telescopes around the world so the skies can be monitored for signals twenty-four hours a day. Argus began with five radio telescopes on April 21, 1996. In June 1999, seventy-nine radio telescopes in sixteen countries were on the team, and more are added every month. When fully operational, Argus will be the first planetwide, coordinated SETI effort.

What If We Succeed?

As astronomers search for intelligent life in the universe, they often ask themselves, "What do we do if we find it?" They also ask, "What do we do if it finds us?"

The SETI Protocol

The SETI Protocol is a set of instructions for SETI teams to follow in the event they pick up an intelligent signal from outer space. The Protocol, an internationally signed agreement, states that the public shall be told immediately if such contact takes place. A panel of distinguished scientists from around the world will then be brought together to decide how to respond to the aliens.

But according to Howard Blum in his book *Out There*, the UFO Working Group (p. 90) obtained a copy of the SETI Protocol in the late 1980s and didn't like what they saw. Members feared that SETI scientists might reveal the existence of Earth to an alien civilization, leaving our planet vulnerable to attack.

In addition, they felt it should not be up to a group of international scientists to represent the planet Earth in communications with aliens. That responsibility, they believed, should fall to the President of the United States.

The UFO Working Group agreed that if an alien message was received by SETI, the U.S. government would instantly clamp a lid of secrecy over the project and take control of the program. Any communication with other planets would happen only under the tightest possible controls.

In his book *Out There,* Blum suggests that in the late 1980s, NASA's SETI program did pick up signals from an advanced civilization—and that thanks to the UFO Working Group, the message is being kept secret from us.

Touch an Alien, Go Directly to Jail!

Federal law 14 CFR, Ch. V, Par. 1211, passed on July 16, 1969, gives NASA the authority to quarantine—in solitary confinement and for as long as it deems necessary—anyone who comes into contact with an extraterrestrial life form.

Some UFO buffs have argued that the law could be used to silence people who have close encounters with aliens. But NASA has explained that the law applies only to astronauts and technicians who handle samples from other planets. It is intended to keep alien bacteria from contaminating Earth and possibly infecting the human race with a deadly virus from space.

Fire Officer's Guide to Disaster Control

FEMA, the Federal Emergency Management Agency, employs thousands of workers who are sent at a moment's notice to assist at disaster areas around the country. In addition, FEMA trains and equips state and local agencies to handle emergency situations.

The *Fire Officer's Guide to Disaster Control* (1993), by former Los Angeles Deputy Fire Chief Charles W. Bahme and William M. Kramer, is FEMA's main textbook for teaching firefighting in connection with a variety of emergencies. In addition to the usual disasters, such as earthquakes, nuclear accidents, and terrorist attacks, the book includes one surprising scenario:

> *"In view of the fact that many ufologists believe that we are fast approaching a time when overt landings of UFOs will become less remarkable, and in the absence of our knowing whether their visits are friendly or hostile, it would not be remiss to give some thought to the part that fire departments might play in the event of the unexpected arrival of UFOs in their communities."*

The manual discusses problems firefighters might encounter when facing a crashed

flying saucer: in addition to heavy traffic and downed communication lines, the authors discuss the psychological impact, the biological danger, how to handle panicking or hysterical crowds, and even difficulties imposed by government attempts to cover up the incident. The authors warn:

> *"...there may be psychological effects produced by force fields that could induce a hypnotic state in the viewer, loss of consciousness, memory lapse, and submission to the occupants."*

The authors conclude the UFO section by suggesting that firefighters approach a downed UFO "with a positive, solicitous [i.e., concerned] attitude of wanting to be of service. This nonaggressive mental state may be telepathically sensed by those aboard or emerging from the craft."

ET TERM:
"EXPERIENCER"

One who has had an abduction experience. Many people who have had such an experience prefer this neutral term over words such as "abductee" or "victim."

Part 4
High Strangeness
(1970s–1980s)

"During the period of 1969–1971... the U.S. government made a deal with these creatures, called EBEs (Extraterrestrial Biological Entities)....The 'deal' was that, in exchange for technology they would provide us, we agreed to ignore the abductions that were going on and suppress information on cattle mutilations."
—statement issued by John Lear, December 29, 1987

ABDUCTION FEVER

It starts when you are alone.

It may happen at home, in bed. You wake from a sound sleep and find you can't move. Your heart is pounding, but you can't cry out.

It may happen outside, in a playground or park, or on a camping trip. You find yourself alone, the rest of your group nowhere in sight. You lose interest in your surroundings. You stand still.

Then the aliens come.

Small beings surround you. They stare at you, fascinated. They begin to touch, poke, and prod you. They guide you to their ship.

Your abduction has begun.

The Abduction Boom

During the 1980s, thousands of people believed they were abducted by aliens. In fact, John E. Mack (p. 107), professor of psychiatry at Harvard University, believes up to 1 million men, women,

---

ALIEN EXPERT: **BUDD HOPKINS**

Budd Hopkins, a painter and sculptor whose work is in the collections of the Guggenheim, Whitney, and many other museums, has been investigating abduction reports for nearly twenty years.

As a young man, Hopkins doubted that flying saucers were real. Then, in 1964, he saw a UFO. In 1975, he learned of a local CE3 case, decided to investigate, and became convinced that the witness was telling the truth. Hopkins investigated his first alien abduction a few years later. He has since come to believe there are tens of thousands—possibly millions—of people who have experienced alien abductions.

---

and children in the United States may have had abduction experiences.

Many abductees have come forward to speak or write about their experiences. Their stories are remarkably similar.

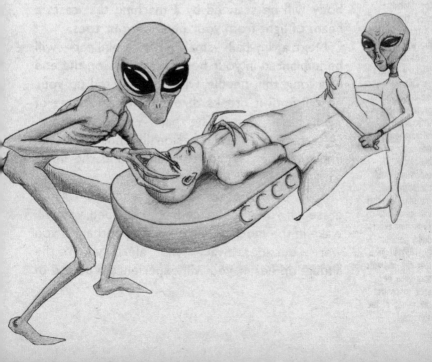

ALIEN FUN FACT: THE IMPLANTS

Although the implant described most often by experiencers is a tiny ball, other shapes (thin slivers, slender tubes, etc.) have also been reported. Ufologists suspect the implants allow the aliens to track people the way human scientists use tracking devices on animals. But the implants may provide aliens with additional information. They may also monitor biological conditions inside the body and transmit thoughts and emotions. Abduction expert Budd Hopkins (p. 105) suggests that the implants may even be used to control the minds of the abductees.

The Abduction Experience

According to many who have purportedly gone through the experience, the following is what will most likely happen if you are abducted by aliens.

First, you will be rendered powerless to resist. Experiencers agree that when you find yourself surrounded by aliens, your body becomes paralyzed and your free will is gone.

Next you will be lifted up by a beam of light—sometimes through solid walls or doors—and "floated" to a waiting spacecraft.

Once on board, you will be placed on a table and examined. Your alien hosts may touch different parts of your body, or they may take tissue samples of your skin. Sometimes your body will be scanned by a machine that casts a beam of light from your head to your toes.

Next, a tiny ball—smaller than a pinhead—will be implanted in your body. The ball is on the end of a long, thin needle, which is inserted up your nostril until it breaks through the membrane of your nasal cavity. The pain will be intense. (Alternate sites are occasionally chosen for the implants, such as the tear ducts and the inner ear.)

Your memories of the entire event will be erased. If you were taken from your bed, you will wake in the morning remembering nothing. If you were outside, awake and alert when the abduction began, you will experience a period of

STAR DATE: JUNE 13–17, 1992—
ABDUCTION CONFERENCE AT MIT

For five days in June 1992, a remarkable meeting took place at the prestigious Massachusetts Institute of Technology. College professors, medical doctors, psychologists, philosophers, physicists, folklorists, experts in scientific analysis, UFO investigators, and a dozen abductees met for a scientific inquiry into abduction accounts. The abductees spent the week discussing their experiences with the experts. Many theories were debated, but at the end of the conference, no conclusion was reached about the objective reality of the abduction experience. The participants agreed, however, that the subject was worthy of scientific study, not ridicule and scorn.

"missing time": you will believe only a moment has passed, while in reality hours have gone by. You may find yourself miles from where you were only an eye-blink before.

You may never remember the abduction, or your memories of the incident may slowly come back—either by themselves, in dreams, or under hypnosis.

ALIEN EXPERT:
JOHN E. MACK, M.D.

Co-chairman of the Abduction Conference at MIT, John E. Mack has been a professor in the Psychiatry Department at the Harvard Medical School for over twenty years, and for a time was head of the department. He is the author of more than 150 scientific papers and won the Pulitzer Prize in 1977. He is also the most renowned defender of the theory that alien abductions are not the product of dreams, sleep paralysis, or hypnosis but are actually occurring as reported. His 1994 book, Abduction, describes how he came to this opinion.

ALIEN FUN FACT: ABDUCTIONS AND AGE

According to folklorist Thomas Bullard (who collects and analyzes alien abduction tales), most experiencers undergo their first abduction at either age seven, between the ages of twelve and thirteen, or between sixteen and seventeen. Bullard claims that if you are not abducted before the age of twenty, your chances of experiencing an alien abduction later in life are slim.

There is one more thing nearly all experiencers agree on: if you are abducted once, you will be abducted again. The aliens will return to abduct and examine you once every few years for the rest of your life.

Why Are Abductions Taking Place?

Why would aliens travel billions of miles to Earth to abduct people? Experiencers and ufologists have proposed several theories:

- Just as human scientists study lab animals, aliens are conducting a long-term study of the human race.
- The aliens—lacking emotions of their own—want to learn more about human emotions.
- The aliens are trying to guide us to a higher level of consciousness.

- The aliens are engaging in genetic experiments for the purpose of creating a hybrid—half alien, half human—race. In fact, many experiencers have reported seeing such hybrid creatures. This has led some investigators to speculate that the aliens come from a dying world and must crossbreed with humans so they can survive here on Earth.

The Skeptics Speak: Dreams and Schemes
Skeptics offer a number of alternate explanations for alien abductions:

- Nighttime abductions are simply very vivid dreams.
- Sleep paralysis (a condition in which a person is unable to move just before falling asleep or just after waking up) and hallucinations are responsible for most abduction experiences.
- Hypnotists plant abduction memories in the minds of abductees.
- Experiencers are mentally unstable and/or seeking attention.

MORE STRANGENESS
The rapid rise in the number of alien abductions in the 1970s and 1980s took UFO researchers by surprise. But that wasn't the only unexpected development in the world of alien encounters.

Cattle Mutilations
During 1973, hundreds of cows grazing on cattle ranches in Minnesota, South Dakota, and Kansas began dying under mysterious circumstances. Parts of the cows' bodies—their tongues, udders, eyes, ears, and certain internal organs—were being

removed with surgical precision, and their bodies drained of blood. In 1974, these cattle mutilations, or "mutes," spread to Nebraska, Oklahoma, and Iowa. By 1975, Colorado was added to the list.

Ufologists suspected that aliens might be involved. There were a number of reasons for this suspicion. As early as 1968, Dr. J. Allen Hynek had interviewed a farmer who claimed a UFO was hovering above his herd of cattle. The farmer believed that the UFO was responsible for the disappearance of some of his cows. And throughout the mid- to late 1970s, flying saucers and nocturnal lights were often reported in the same areas where the cattle mutilations occurred. For instance, in one Colorado county, ranchers claimed a huge red saucer appeared two or three days before the cattle mutilations began. Were aliens conducting experiments on cattle?

Cattle mutilations continue to be reported all over the world to the present day.

The Skeptics Speak: Mute Evidence

In 1979, the FBI established the Animal Mutilation Project, a

---

ALIEN EXPERT:
LINDA MOULTON HOWE

Linda Moulton Howe is an award-winning investigative reporter and documentary filmmaker who has produced more than three hundred television programs. Howe first became intrigued with cattle mutilations—and their possible connection to UFOs—during the 1970s. Her television documentary on the subject, Strange Harvest, was broadcast nationally on May 25, 1980. Howe went on to produce more television documentaries on paranormal and environmental themes. In 1993, she produced a follow-up documentary, Strange Harvests 1993, which attempted to prove that the mysterious mutilations were still occurring.

task force assigned to investigate the mutilations. The task force declared the mystery solved a year later: the cattle were dying of natural causes. The mutilated condition of the bodies was caused by animal scavengers, such as coyotes and buzzards, and the normal process of decomposition.

Ranchers familiar with the effects of predators and scavengers scoff at the FBI's explanation. They claim that the bureau didn't examine the mutilated cows at all, but spent all their time studying animals that had died of natural causes.

Crop Circles

Crop circles are enormous patterns made of flattened plants in fields of wheat, barley, and tall grasses.

The first crop circles were discovered by English farmers in 1980. They were simple, large, round, flattened areas. Over the years, however, the discovered patterns have become much more

Geometric crop circle seen at Liddington Castle in southern England in 1999.

Precisely formed crop circle seen at Littlebury
Castle in southern England in 1997.

complex—rings within rings, geometric shapes, and intricate designs. Many crop circle investigators, or cerealogists (seer-ee-AHL-uh-jists), believe these elaborate patterns may be messages in an alien alphabet.

From 1980 to 1987, fewer than one hundred crop circles were found around the world. But in 1988 alone, over one hundred were discovered worldwide. In 1990, more than one thousand were found.

Some scientists speculate that crop circles may be created by a rare atmospheric occurrence called a plasma vortex, a small, electrically charged whirlwind. These whirlwinds whip an enormous amount of energy toward the ground, where it spreads out, causing vegetation to bend over. A plasma vortex, however, would account for only the simplest round crop circles.

The Skeptics Speak: Turning in Circles

Skeptics dismiss all crop circles (except, possibly, simple round ones) as hoaxes. In fact, two elderly gentlemen in England publicly claimed responsibility for starting the craze by producing the majority of the crop patterns in

Great Britain during the 1980s. Cerealogists have rebutted their claim as absurd, characterizing the two men as attention-seekers.

Cerealogists acknowledge that a great number of crop circles are hoaxes, but they believe they can tell the difference between a genuine circle and a faked one just by the condition of the plants. For example, they claim that the stalks in a "real" crop circle are gently bent over, while those in a hoaxed circle are stomped flat and broken. Some crop circles proclaimed "genuine" by cerealogists have later been proven to be hoaxes.

The Face on Mars

On July 31, 1976, NASA released photos of Mars taken by *Viking 1*, a U.S. satellite launched to study the planet. One photo showed an area scientists named Cydonia (sy-DOH-nyuh). In their description of the photo, NASA noted that a "huge rock formation in the center, which resembles a human head, is formed by shadows giving the illusion of eyes, nose, and mouth." NASA humorously dubbed the rock "The Face on Mars."

But was the face an illusion? In the 1980s, two scientists at the Goddard Spaceflight Center—Vincent DiPietro and Gregory Molenaar—decided to study the image. They compared it to another photo of the same area taken from a different angle. The Face was still there. It was not a trick of light and shadow, DiPietro and Molenaar concluded, but an actual, mile-wide formation in the shape of a human face.

So who created—or what caused—The Face? Natural forces, such as erosion? Or was it built by an alien civilization as a cosmic greeting to earthlings?

DiPietro and Molenaar's work prompted other researchers to examine rock formations in the Cydonia region. Richard Hoagland (p. 115), a former NASA consultant who has spent years analyzing the *Viking 1* photos, claims he has found evidence of intelligent design in a group of landforms near The Face, which he has dubbed "The City."

Cydonia and the *Mars Global Surveyor*

Many UFO researchers feel that more study is required to determine if The Face and the other "monuments" on Mars are alien artifacts or natural geological features.

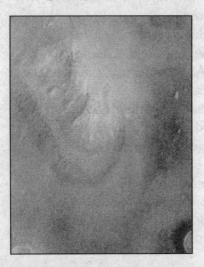

This *Mars Global Surveyor* close-up image of the "face" feature of the Cydonia region has been filtered and contrast-enhanced.

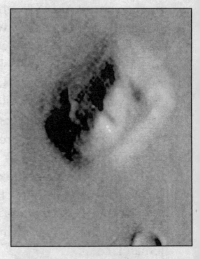

Additional photographic techniques were used to produce this enhanced image of the "face" on Mars.

As it happens, such study has already begun. In 1998, NASA's *Mars Global Surveyor* went into orbit around Mars. The Mars Orbital Camera (MOC), mounted on the satellite, is now taking detailed, high-resolution photographs of the planet's surface. At least one photograph of The Face has already been transmitted to Earth.

So far, nothing conclusive has been determined from the photo. It looks less like a face than in the *Viking 1* photos, but the MOC image was partially obscured by a disturbance in the Martian atmosphere.

ALIEN EXPERT:
RICHARD HOAGLAND

Richard Hoagland has served as a consultant for NASA and was a science adviser for <u>CBS News</u> during the <u>Apollo</u> moon missions in the 1960s and 1970s. Hoagland was also instrumental in persuading NASA to attach the "greeting" to <u>Pioneer 10</u> and <u>11</u> in the early 1970s (p. 94). In 1984, Hoagland founded "The Mars Project," a group of scientists dedicated to solving the riddle of The Face on Mars. Hoagland's book <u>The Monuments of Mars</u> (1987) outlines in detail his theories about The Face and other structures on Mars.

The Skeptics Speak: The Farce on Mars

Most planetary geologists believe the "face" and other "monuments" on Mars are natural surface features, formed millions of years ago by Mars-quakes, wind erosion, and possibly running water. However, even these scientists agree that it is important to study the Cydonia region for what the area reveals about Mars's geological past.

MORE UFO HOAXES

From the beginning of the flying saucer era in the late 1940s, hoaxes have confounded the study of UFO and alien encounters. Although the actual number of proven hoaxes is quite small, they complicate the ufologist's job tremendously. An investigator may spend months or years studying a particularly interesting case, only to find that the entire incident was a hoax. How can a researcher tell a hoaxer from a sincere witness, a skillful prank from a genuinely puzzling encounter? It isn't easy.

These three UFO incidents received a lot of publicity when they occurred in the 1970s and 1980s. All three turned out to be hoaxes.

Beamship from the Pleiades

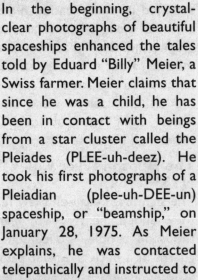

In the beginning, crystal-clear photographs of beautiful spaceships enhanced the tales told by Eduard "Billy" Meier, a Swiss farmer. Meier claims that since he was a child, he has been in contact with beings from a star cluster called the Pleiades (PLEE-uh-deez). He took his first photographs of a Pleiadian (plee-uh-DEE-un) spaceship, or "beamship," on January 28, 1975. As Meier explains, he was contacted telepathically and instructed to

meet the ship in a meadow near his farm in Hinwill, Switzerland. The ship landed, a door opened, and out stepped the beautiful Pleiadian female Semjase. According to Meier, Semjase revealed to him the history and future of the universe along with the meaning of life. Over the next few years, Meier took hundreds of photographs of the beamships, many of which were published in a handsome volume.

Soon people were coming from all over the world to meet with Meier and hear him speak. Meier provided metal samples from the beamship to a research scientist at IBM for analysis. The scientist said they were like nothing he had ever seen on Earth.

But Meier's claims were soon challenged. The subtitle of Kal Korff's 1981 book, *The Meier Incident,* summed up the situation nicely: *The Most Infamous Hoax in Ufology.* Digital analysis of Meier's photographs indicated that they were pictures of small models rather than large spacecraft; further analysis revealed strings and rods holding up the models. The models themselves were later found in Meier's home, along with obviously faked pictures that Meier had begun to destroy.

The Hudson River Valley "Siege" (1983–1984)

The sightings began on New Year's Eve, 1983. Before they ended, nearly two years later, almost five thousand people—policemen, housewives, security guards at a nuclear power plant, IBM engineers, and schoolteachers—had seen the Hudson River Valley UFO.

According to these witnesses, the UFO was shaped like a giant boomerang, with lights running along the underside; it was an enormous flying "V" that blocked out the stars as it passed overhead. Some people who watched the UFO through binoculars claimed they could clearly see the structure to which the lights were attached. One witness, Philip J. Imbrogno, interviewed many other witnesses and co-wrote a book about the events with J. Allen Hynek, *Night Siege: The Hudson Valley UFO Sightings* (1987).

UFO debunkers had a field day when they discovered a group of pilots of "ultra-light" aircraft who were flying over the Hudson River Valley area at night. The ultra-light pilots, it turned out, were playing a hoax on the residents of the valley. Because the flew their aircraft close together in a "V" formation, the lights on the planes created the illusion of the giant, boomerang-shaped UFO.

But was this the complete answer? There is no doubt that many of the witnesses had seen the hoaxed UFO. But many other witnesses reported an object that could hover in place for several minutes, fly in total silence, and move with tremendous bursts of speed—all feats beyond the capability of ultra-light aircraft. Some UFO investigators remain convinced that this second group of witnesses saw an actual UFO.

The Gulf Breeze Sightings

On November 11, 1987, Ed Walters, a businessman in Gulf Breeze, Florida, began taking snapshots of a UFO he claimed was floating above his backyard. According to Walters, a beam of blue light suddenly flashed down from the craft, paralyzing his body and lifting him momentarily into the air. After a few moments, the blue light clicked off, he fell to the ground, and the UFO flew away. Walters was confused and upset. The next day, he anonymously mailed the photos—clear, sharp pictures of a flying saucer—to the local newspaper.

A few days later, the UFO came back. This time Walters heard a computer-like voice in his head, which he believed was coming from the UFO. Walters took additional pictures of the craft, even though the voice told him not to.

Walters and his wife claimed they had many more encounters with the UFO, which began addressing Ed as "Zehaas." Walters and his wife went on to write *The Gulf Breeze Sightings* (1990), a national bestseller illustrated with his photographs.

But it was a hoax. After the book was published, Walters's story began to unravel. A local teenager came forward and admitted that Walters had asked him to help fake the photos. In the attic of Walters's house, a reporter found the model of the UFO used in the fake photos.

Walters's hoax may have been inspired by the fact that people in the Gulf Breeze area had been reporting strange lights in the sky for years. No one besides Walters and his wife, however, saw the flying saucer depicted in his photographs. Many investigators now believe the mysterious lights seen by other people were caused by test flights of secret aircraft from a nearby military base.

CONSPIRACY THEORIES

Is the government hiding what it knows about aliens? Some UFO researchers, such as Jacques Vallee (p.144), think that government officials are simply hiding the fact that they don't know any more about UFOs than we do. But others see a sinister, far-reaching conspiracy to hide, as they put it, the "horrible truth."

MJ-12

In 1984, an anonymous source gave two UFO investigators a top-secret document. When the investigators made the papers public two and a half years later, their revelations made headlines around the world.

On the evening of December 11, 1984, TV producer Jaime Shandera found a large envelope stuffed into his mailbox. Inside was a roll of undeveloped film. Suspecting that it was somehow connected to his recent research into UFOs, Shandera brought the film to his friend, UFO investigator William Moore. When they developed it together, they found photographs of startling government papers.

The "MJ-12 document," as it came to be called, appeared to be a top-secret presidential briefing memo from 1952 about the Roswell, New Mexico, flying saucer crash (p. 26). At the top of each page were emblazoned the words "TOP-SECRET" and

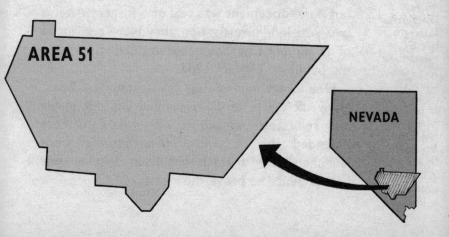

AREA 51

NEVADA

ET TERM:
E.B.E.

The initials E.B.E. stand for "Extraterrestrial Biological Entity," a technical name for an alien being. The term first appeared in the MJ-12 document. Even though that document has been proven a hoax, some UFO investigators still use these initials to refer to any alien. The original E.B.E. was purportedly the sole alien survivor of the Roswell crash. According to some UFO researchers, the being—nick-named "Ebe" (EE-bee) by the Air Force colonel guarding it— lived at the Army base at Los Alamos until its death from unknown causes in 1952.

"EYES ONLY." The document was apparently written to make then newly elected President Eisenhower aware of what the government knew about UFOs. In brief, that:

- A real flying saucer had crashed in Roswell in July of 1947.
- Three dead aliens—along with one live one— were recovered from the crash site.
- A twelve-member panel made up of military officers, government scientists, and intelligence agents—code-named "Majestic-12"— had been formed by order of President Truman in 1947 to study the aliens and their technology.

This was it—the document ufologists had long dreamed of finding. If the document was genuine, it would prove that one of the most important events in human history had occurred. It would also prove that the government had been hiding the truth about UFOs for almost forty years.

Moore and Shandera were determined to find out if the document was real or a forgery. After a two-year-long investigation, they were convinced of its authenticity. They released the document to the public on May 29, 1987.

Debunkers immediately proclaimed it a hoax. Many ufologists carefully studied the document and reluctantly agreed it was a fake. Others defended the document. Investigations were launched on both sides, with each claiming they had evidence to prove their case.

Finally, in 1989, conclusive evidence surfaced. Debunker Philip Klass discovered that President Truman's signature on the MJ-12 document was an exact copy of his signature on an earlier letter. Since no can sign their name exactly the same way twice, this was convincing evidence that the document had indeed been forged.

Klass's discovery left a looming question: who had created the false document? Government experts say only someone with extensive knowledge of top-secret military files could have made the MJ-12 document look so convincing. Why would someone with that knowledge go to all the trouble? Was it simply a prank? Or was it, as some investigators

U.S. SIGNS TREATY WITH SPACE ALIENS!

The strangest, most convoluted conspiracy theory of all time goes like this: shortly after the crash at Roswell, a flying saucer landed at Edwards Air Force Base in California. The aliens aboard struck a deal with the U.S. government. In exchange for alien technological information, the government gave the aliens permission to abduct people and mutilate cattle.

According to this theory, underneath heavily guarded military installations throughout the U.S. are huge subterranean cities where millions of aliens work on horrific experiments. These include implanting mind-control devices in humans, transplanting alien brains into human bodies, and growing human flesh (which the aliens must consume in order to survive) in giant vats.

While thousands of UFO buffs believe the theory is true, few UFO researchers take any of it very seriously. Jerome Clark, editor of *The UFO Encyclopedia*, calls the theory a "bad joke." Jacques Vallee agrees, calling it the "best horror story" he has heard since he was a child.

propose, a deliberate attempt by the government to confuse and befuddle UFO researchers? And if so, why?

"Dreamland"

The Nellis Test Range in Nevada is one of the most tightly guarded military installations in the world. Area 51 at Nellis, known as "Dreamland," is also one of the most secret. For years, the government denied that it even existed.

Area 51 is built on the vast bed of Groom Dry Lake. It consists of a bewildering array of giant hangars, observation towers, support facilities, and what might be the longest runway in the world. Secret military aircraft have been developed and tested there since the 1950s.

And according to many UFO researchers, Area 51 is where the U.S. military conducts tests on aircraft based on alien technology. Witnesses claim they have seen aircraft perform aerial feats above the base—loops, sharp turns, accelerating from hovering to blistering speed in the blink

---

ALIEN EXPERT: JOHN LEAR

The leading proponent of the underground base conspiracy theory is John Lear, son of the inventor of the Learjet. Lear is a top-notch pilot who holds several world speed records and has flown secret missions for the CIA. He became interested in UFOs and alien abductions during the 1980s and investigated several incidents. Lear claims his information regarding the alien bases comes from contacts within U.S. government intelligence agencies. In December 1987, Lear released a lengthy statement outlining the history of the underground bases and the alien treaties.

PLACES TO VISIT: THE EXTRATERRESTRIAL HIGHWAY

Over the years, thousands of UFO buffs have traveled down a Nevada highway called "State Route 375." This stretch of road is the closest the public can come to Area 51. On April 18, 1996, Nevada renamed part of the road "The Extraterrestrial Highway."

Not all UFO investigators were happy about the new name. Some thought it trivialized a serious issue. But most local residents looked forward to the tourists they hoped the new moniker would attract. The Nevada Commission on Tourism even created a club for people who drive the ET Highway. Members get a glow-in-the-dark license plate frame reading "I Was Out There," a T-shirt, a lapel pin, an "I Was Out There" bumper sticker, and a subscription to "Eyes Only," the club's newsletter.

---

of an eye—that would be impossible for any conventional craft.

Even the conservative industry journal *Aviation Week & Space Technology* reported in 1990 that extraordinary aircraft had been sighted over Area 51. These included triangular craft, noiseless craft, and aircraft that rely on "exotic" propulsion systems, possibly including anti-gravity devices.

S-4

Area 51, as big as it is, is only one part of the much larger Nellis Test Range complex, which covers over 8 million acres. According to Robert Lazar, who claims he worked there as a propulsion engineer, one area of Nellis is even more tightly guarded than Area 51: a section designated as S-4.

According to Lazar, S-4 contains a group of hangars carved into a mountain, and stored in those hangars are nine alien flying saucers. Lazar claims that the Air Force is taking the saucers apart to learn how they work—a process called "reverse engineering." Lazar says he was allowed to crawl inside one of the saucers and touch the controls. But when he violated his security clearance by telling his wife and some friends what he was doing, he was kicked off the project.

The Skeptics Speak: Bizarre Lazar

Robert Lazar's story has been categorically denied by the U.S. military. It has also been questioned by many UFO investigators. For one thing, it seems that Lazar lied about his past: there is no proof that he ever attended the schools or held the jobs he says he did. Lazar and his supporters claim that his past has been "erased" by intelligence agencies.

Many investigators also feel that details of Lazar's story make no sense. For instance, before he was supposedly recruited for the most covert and possibly significant job in human history, he was managing a photo shop.

MEET TODAY'S ALIENS

As in the 1950s and 1960s, today's ufologists make an effort to catalog and categorize reports of alien encounters. However, there seems to be little agreement among ufologists as to the number of alien races turning up in recent witness reports. Some ufologists believe witnesses are describing four distinct alien races. Others believe nine races are being reported. Others claim there are twelve. One author puts the number as high as seventy! Following are the alien races that appear most frequently in today's witness reports:

Grays
Witnesses have described three different types of gray-skinned aliens.

Common Grays
These humanoid aliens stand three and a half to four and a half feet tall. Slender and frail with thin limbs, they have heads that are large and completely hairless. They have a lipless slit for a mouth, pointed chins, no ears, and no nose—just two nostril holes. Most memorable of their features are their enormous black, "hypnotic" eyes. Some ufologists speculate that these blank black lenses are really protective coverings over their actual eyes.

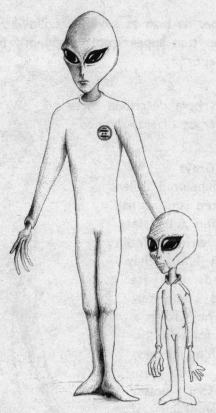

Tall Grays
Less frequently reported than common Grays, these aliens stand five to five and a half feet tall. Occasionally, they are reported to have a pronounced nose. Some abductees report that tall Grays seem to be in charge of common Grays. Witnesses claim to have seen the taller gray aliens giving orders to their shorter companions, much as a high-ranking military officer would give instructions to an underling.

Small Gray
Shorter and heavier than the common Gray, this type of alien is reported even less frequently than the tall Gray. When they are seen, however, they are usually wearing a helmet and body armor. They seem to be more militaristic in nature than the common or tall Grays, and may in fact be soldiers or guards. Some abductees think they might even be robots.

"Nordics"
Human-looking beings, usually over six feet tall, with blond hair and piercing blue eyes. These aliens are called "Nordics" due to their resemblance to humans from Scandinavia or northern Europe. Both males and females are described as being extremely attractive. Their eyes are sometimes described as catlike, or slanting. Kind, patient, and loving, Nordics are often dressed in militaristic uniforms. Abductees

occasionally report encountering Nordics in the company of common Grays. Nordics were the type of alien most often reported by the contactees, and as such they are sometimes referred to as "Venusians" (p. 32).

Reptoids

Reptoids (short for "reptilian humanoids") are lizard-like creatures with scaled skin and faces, like dinosaurs. They can be up to eight feet tall. Their hands are clawlike, and their golden eyes have black slits for pupils. Some researchers theorize that these aliens may be intelligent descendants of the dinosaurs. Rarely encountered, Reptoids are felt to be sinister and not trustworthy by people who claim to have seen them.

Blues

These rarely seen humanoid beings possess slightly bluish translucent skin and almond-shaped eyes. They stand approximately five and a half feet tall.

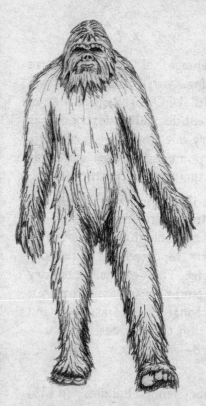

Hairy Hominids

Some sightings of large, hairy, apelike creatures such as Sasquatch ("Bigfoot") and Yeti ("The Abominable Snowman") have been linked with UFO sightings. This has led some researchers to speculate that these beings are actually alien

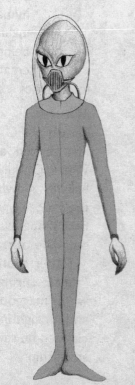

entities. Most investigators, however, are not ready to categorically identify these creatures as aliens.

Giants or "Talls"

Rarely reported, giant aliens stand between seven and ten feet tall. They are usually seen wearing one-piece coveralls; occasionally, helmets and breathing apparatuses complete the outfit.

"Smalls"

A tiny percentage of witnesses have reported seeing very small aliens in connection with UFO sightings. Some of these small entities are described as resembling fairy-tale gnomes—small, ugly creatures with pointy ears. Other witnesses have reported tiny human-looking beings.

Non-Humanoid: Monsters, Energy Forms, and Interdimensionals

The rarest and arguably the most terrifying alien encounters reported are with non-humanoid aliens. This catchall category includes amorphous, shapeless creatures; beings that change shape at will; and creatures that can only be described as—for want of a better word—monsters.

Monsters

British UFO researcher Jenny Randles (p.135) investigated a case involving a youth in central Wales. On July 22, 1975, the boy saw a large, round, brightly glowing saucer on the ground. The top of the saucer was a clear dome, and inside the boy saw two shapeless, quivering creatures who seemed to be made of transparent jelly.

Other examples include an incident in Yssandon, France, during which drivers reported seeing giant white maggots crossing a road near a landed UFO; and a sighting in Spain, when a chicken farmer claimed he saw two "octopus-like" beings run into a spaceship.

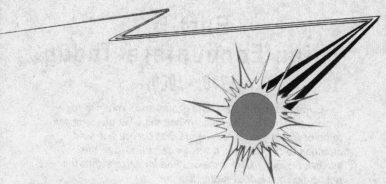

Energy Forms

Some witnesses have described entities that can only be compared to raw energy. Sometimes these creatures appear as floating balls of light. Jenny Randles believes such entities may be something like giant amoebas (one-celled microscopic creatures).

Interdimensionals

Phantoms, or ghostlike apparitions, are occasionally reported in connection with UFO sightings. Sometimes these entities are seen walking through walls or fences. They have been reported most often by passengers in moving cars who see these beings on the road. Randles has dubbed these entities "inter-dimensionals" and theorizes that they don't come from outer space but from another dimension.

Part 5
Alien Encounters Today
(1990s–2000s)

"...journalists and professional debunkers... continue to declare that 'science' had determined the UFO phenomenon to be bogus. In fact, to the degree that science has paid attention to the problem, it has tended to validate the intuitive feeling of UFO witnesses and lay citizens that the phenomenon is indeed a puzzling one."
—Jerome Clark, *The UFO Encyclopedia*, v. 1 (1990)

RECENT SIGHTINGS AND CLOSE ENCOUNTERS

More than fifty years after Kenneth Arnold's 1947 sighting ushered in the modern age of flying saucers, the UFO mystery continues to resist an easy solution. Close encounters of the first, second, and third kind are today reported regularly throughout the world, and UFO flaps have occurred in every populated country. Even as debunkers insist there is no UFO mystery, the ranks of puzzled, sometimes frightened, witnesses continue to grow.

North America

Hundreds of UFO sightings were reported during every year of the 1990s; this is just a small sample:

On February 5, 1992, about fifty people saw a huge object shaped like a boomerang fly over the Susquehanna Valley in Pennsylvania.

On December 21, 1994, two neighbors in Kingsley, Michigan, caught a brightly glowing barrel-shaped UFO on video. The sighting was also witnessed by a policeman and several other individuals.

In February 1995, dozens of people saw two green-glowing boomerang-shaped UFOs flying over Ross, California.

On August 22, 1996, CNN reported that scientists videotaping a thunderstorm in Kansas caught a bright ball of light on the tape. The object, traveling in the Earth's upper atmosphere, was moving at roughly 1/100th the speed of light—an incredible 7 million miles an hour. What the object was is still unknown.

On November 16, 1996, the pilots of two commercial jets both reported the same UFO over Long Island, New York. The FAA (Federal Aviation Administration) responded by closing that air lane for several hours.

On March 13, 1997, thousands of residents throughout Arizona saw six bright lights moving in formation over the state. Videotapes of the mystery

---

ALIEN EXPERT: JENNY RANDLES

Jenny Randles is the director of investigations for BUFORA (the British UFO Research Association). She is the author of fifteen books on UFOs. Randles believes that at least 95% of reported sightings have conventional explanations. It is the remaining 5%, she argues, that cannot be explained without acknowledging the existence of something beyond our understanding.

The "Oz Factor" is a phrase Randles coined to describe the dreamlike state UFO witnesses often say they experience during an encounter. It is described as a sensation of being transported from the normal, everyday world into a slightly different reality.

roswell

ALIEN FUN FACT: POLL NUMBERS

In a 1991 Roper Poll, 7% of American adults believed they had seen a UFO at some time in their lives. This equals almost 17½ million sightings.

lights, made by witnesses in Scottsdale, Tempe, Tucson, and Phoenix, were aired on the local TV news.

On April 22, 1998, more than a dozen people in different parts of Washington state reported a bright blue-green object flying through the sky, changing speed and direction, and executing aerial maneuvers.

On June 18, 1999, eight witnesses in Watkins Glen, New York, saw an object in the sky that resembled a spinning "silver disco ball." The distant object drifted across the sky for several minutes, until it made a sudden ninety-degree turn and accelerated so quickly it vanished within a second.

On January 5, 2000, police officers and other witnesses in Millstadt, Lebanon, Shiloh, and Du Quoin, Illinois, reported seeing a gigantic, arrowhead-shaped UFO fly silently overhead.

According to one of the witnesses, the object was the length of a football field and three stories high.

Worldwide UFO Flaps

Although the United States has not had a nationwide UFO flap since 1974, there were several full-fledged flaps in other countries during the 1990s.

Belgium's Black Triangles (1989–1991)

From 1989 to 1991, the tiny European country of Belgium experienced one of the most intense UFO flaps in history as hundreds of witnesses reported seeing black triangular objects in the skies. In 1991 alone, over two thousand of these sightings were reported. The objects were able to execute seemingly impossible maneuvers, such as going from high speeds to full stops in midair. Several witnesses took videotapes of the black triangles.

The Belgian Ministry of Defense officially acknowledged the problem in 1990. On the night of

March 30, 1990, two F-16 fighters attempted to intercept three of the unidentified objects. The jets locked their radar on the objects, but the UFOs, which had been cruising slowly, suddenly burst ahead at a fantastic speed. The radar tape from one of the F-16s was released to the public, and any conventional explanations—such as temperature inversions or testing of secret man-made aircraft—were ruled out.

The Skeptics Speak: Belgian Waffles

Doubt was cast on the Belgian wave by scientists at the Astrophysical Institute at the University of Liège, in Belgium. From the beginning of the flap in 1989, they were on the lookout for the black triangular UFOs, but they claim they saw nothing out of the ordinary. The scientists analyzed several reports and videos, and determined the triangles to be caused either by Venus or by the lights of ordinary airplanes.

Mexico City's UFO Videos (1991)

The single most-videotaped UFO sighting of all time occurred on July 11, 1991. A total eclipse of the sun had been predicted for Mexico City, and many people had their camcorders ready. A news crew for Televisa, the Mexican television network, was also standing by to videotape the event. When the sun was completely covered by the moon, a brilliant silver disk-shaped object appeared from beneath the hidden sun. That night, Televisa's startling video was broadcast on TV. By the end of the week, sixteen more videotapes were submitted from viewers all over the city who had also caught the UFO on tape. According to UFO investigators, analysis of the tapes ruled out Venus or a bright star as the cause of the UFO.

Over the next few months, this sighting was followed by a wave of hundreds of sightings over Mexico City. Witnesses submitted videotapes of these UFOs as well. Although some were obvious hoaxes, many seemed to show genuinely puzzling phenomena. At one point during the wave, Mexico

City's airport had to be closed for an hour due to UFOs in the sky above the runways.

Scotland's Sightings (1992–1997)
Scotland was the site of a UFO flap from 1992 to 1997. Over two thousand sightings were reported, including red and orange balls, black disks with red and green lights, and traditional flying saucers. One family of three claimed they saw an object the size of a house land on the ground near them, and that they were then chased by another UFO that had been circling overhead.

Canada's Flap (1994–1995)
Canada experienced a surge in sightings from 1994 to 1995. Among the hundreds of unexplained objects reported to the police and Air Force were an object shaped like an arrowhead that appeared to be three times larger than a 747, a doughnut-shaped object with flashing lights, four copper cigar-shaped objects, and two brightly glowing objects that pursued a car.

Cuba Breaks Its Silence (1995)
In October of 1995, a wave of UFO sightings were reported in Cuba. This was the first time that the government-controlled media on that island were allowed to report any UFO sightings in Cuba.

The first sighting occurred on October 15, 1995. A seventy-four-year-old farmer claimed a

SPACE SHUTTLE SIGHTING

Astronauts aboard the space shuttle have seen their fair share of unidentified objects in space. One such incident was captured on videotape by the shuttle astronauts on September 15, 1991. On the tape, several glowing objects can be seen in motion outside the shuttle's window. Some of the objects quickly change direction and then shoot away from the shuttle. NASA scientists explained that the glowing objects were actually ice crystals dislodged by a firing thruster. But some UFO researchers have pointed out problems with this explanation. The objects seem to be moving too quickly, they say, and the theory can't account for the way some of them change direction. These researchers insist the objects must be classified as UFOs.

bell-shaped UFO landed on his farm. The farmer saw two entities—one who remained in the ship, and a second being in a space suit who exited the craft and collected plant samples from the farmer's field. Finally, the creature returned to the ship, which immediately took off. The farmer called the police and described what he had seen. Shortly afterward, representatives from the Cuban intelligence agency arrived and found footprints and burn marks.

Many more UFOs were seen over Cuba during the next few weeks. Among the witnesses were several platoons of Cuban soldiers.

Worldwide Flap (1996)

In 1996, a worldwide flap of sightings occurred.

It began in Brazil in January and continued for eleven months until November. All the classic UFO shapes were reported—bright lights, giant cigars, and black triangles. An unusual report involved a giant rectangle, which was seen by some three hundred witnesses, one of whom said it looked like a twenty-story building laid on its side.

Australia's flap began in June. Among the thousands of witnesses were scores of Air Force personnel and police. Most of the UFOs seen were bright orange lights, which danced individually and in groups in the sky. The same lights were also seen flying in formation.

Israel was hit by a flap of sightings in July and August. These included multicolored lights that danced in the night sky.

A Canadian flap began in October with a number of sightings in Manitoba. A variety of objects were seen, including a giant hexagon and an upside-down bowl.

The Great Flap of China (1999)

From September through December of 1999, hundreds of people in Beijing, Shanghai, and other major cities in China reported seeing unidentified orange-yellow glowing objects moving through the sky. Witnesses ranged from laborers to college deans. Many of the objects were videotaped, and the images are now being enthusiastically studied by engineers and scientists, along with members of China's Air Force.

ALTERNATE THEORIES

Most people are aware of only two explanations for UFOs: that they are alien spacecraft, or that they are ordinary objects and/or natural phenomena mistaken for alien spacecraft.

But in fact, modern UFO researchers have several other theories under consideration.

"Folklore in the Making"

Some researchers have been struck by the parallels between ancient folklore—the traditional tales and beliefs of a culture—and modern UFO encounters. These researchers speculate that another level of reality—possibly another dimension—overlaps our own. Occasionally, it is speculated, beings from this other reality intrude into our world. And when this happens, we interpret the event in terms we can understand.

Our ancestors called these creatures fairies, goblins, and trolls, and attempted to describe them and their behaviors as best they could. Today we "know" that such quaint creatures do not exist. As theorist Kenneth Ring put it, "fairies are out of style." We live in the Space Age—so now we see "space aliens" from another planet. The beings are the same—but their form has changed to fit our expectations.

PARALLELS TO FOLKLORE

JACQUES VALLEE BELIEVES THAT THE PARALLELS BETWEEN COMMON
UFO EXPERIENCES AND FOLKLORE ARE TOO NUMEROUS TO IGNORE.

FOLKLORE	UFO ENCOUNTERS
FAIRIES, ELVES, GOBLINS, ETC. COMMONLY DESCRIBED AS BEING THREE AND A HALF FEET TALL.	Aliens often described as being about three and a half feet tall.
SYLPHS FLEW INSIDE "CLOUDSHIPS" WITH THE SPEED OF LIGHTNING.	Flying saucers fly through the air at the speed of light.
FAIRIES AND ELVES STEAL CROPS AND CATTLE.	Aliens take plant samples and mutilate cattle.
FAIRIES ACCUSED OF ABDUCTING MEN, WOMEN, AND CHILDREN.	Aliens accused of abducting men, women, and children.
FAIRIES INTERESTED IN PREGNANT WOMEN.	Aliens interested in pregnant women.
SUPERNATURAL RACES WOULD ABDUCT AND THEN MARRY HUMANS IN ORDER TO HAVE HYBRID CHILDREN TO IMPROVE THEIR STOCK.	Aliens abduct humans to create hybrid children to save their species.
WOMEN BELIEVED THEIR BABIES WERE STOLEN AND REPLACED BY "CHANGELINGS" (FAIRY OR GOBLIN BABIES).	Women believe their unborn babies are stolen; often later shown children who are half alien/half human.
MANY TALES OF PEOPLE WHO THOUGHT THEY WERE WITH THE FAIRY FOLK FOR ONLY HOURS WHEN YEARS OR DECADES HAD PASSED.	"Missing time"—people think they were gone only minutes when hours or days have passed.
FAIRIES OCCASIONALLY USED PARALYSIS TO CONTROL HUMANS.	Aliens sometimes use paralysis to control humans.
VISIBLE SCAR OR MARK AFTER BEING VISITED BY DEMONS.	Visible scar or mark after being visited by aliens.

ALIEN EXPERT: JACQUES VALLEE

Jacques Vallee first became interested in UFOs when, as a young astronomer in France, he and several colleagues tracked a number of mysterious objects in the sky. The objects were moving in ways impossible for conventional aircraft. However, Vallee became even more interested in the reaction of his superiors at the observatory. Rather than responding with curiosity, they denied the observations ever took place. Vallee's supervisors destroyed the observatory's films and records of the sighting and then claimed that the objects were nothing but ordinary airplanes or planets.

Vallee developed an interest in how human beings interpret and process information and eventually became an expert in creating computer databases. In the 1960s, as a graduate student at Northwestern University, Vallee met J. Allen Hynek, and they became colleagues and friends.

Vallee's greatest claim to fame, however, may be that he was the model for the French UFO investigator in Steven Spielberg's film <u>Close Encounters of the Third Kind</u>.

Scholars of folklore and philosophy have named the alternate reality these beings inhabit the "imaginal" (ih-MA-juh-nul) realm. Don't confuse "imaginal" with "imaginary." The imaginal, they suggest, is a real place. We cannot access it through our ordinary senses, but under rare conditions we are able to see and even enter it. The beings who live there, on the other hand, seem to be able to enter our world at will.

Jacques Vallee is one of the leading advocates of this theory. Vallee doesn't believe that UFOs can be explained as simple "nuts-and-bolts" spaceships flying here from other planets. Instead, he believes that inhabitants of a parallel universe are poking their way into ours, and have been since before recorded history.

Can such an alternate reality really exist? Today's most advanced research into quantum physics suggests that rather than the three dimensions we are conscious of (height, width, and depth), the universe might actually consist of many more dimensions. Some theorists suggest as many as twenty-seven!

Tectonic Stress Theory and "Earthlights" Theory

These two similar theories suggest that UFOs are the result of natural processes that occur regularly beneath the Earth's crust.

Tectonic Stress Theory (or TST) was first proposed by Michael Persinger, a professor of neuroscience and psychology at Laurentian University, in Ontario, Canada. In a series of articles published in the scholarly journal *Perceptual and Motor Skills,* Persinger theorized that when the Earth's crust undergoes the normal stresses and strains that produce earth-quakes, electromagnetic radiation is released into the environment. Persinger believes that this radiation has two effects: first, it creates glowing lights in the air, which people see as UFOs. Secondly, it directly affects people's brain waves, causing them to believe they are seeing all sorts of unusual things, from flying saucers to alien beings.

The "Earthlights" theory is a similar idea, proposed by Paul Devereux, a researcher and self-described "cognitive archaeologist." In 1967, Devereux himself saw a bright orange rectangle of light in the sky. Soon after that experience, he formulated his theory and began his research, compiling the results in his 1982 book *Earthlights.*

ALIEN FUN FACT: PATENT PENDING

Between 1957 and 1965, eight scientists applied for—and received—United States patents for disk-shaped flying aircraft. Some researchers who believe UFOs are man-made point to these patents as evidence for their case.

Like Persinger, Devereux believes that pressure building up in the Earth can cause lights to appear. But his theory only explains nocturnal lights. Daylight disks and close encounters, Devereux believes, are misidentifications, delusions, or hoaxes.

Both Persinger and Devereux have conducted detailed studies that seem to prove that UFO activity increases before major earthquakes. If true, these findings would help support their theories.

Gas Plasmas (or "Ball Lightning")

Aviation writer and UFO debunker Philip J. Klass was the first to propose the gas plasma theory to explain UFO sightings. At one time Klass believed that this theory was the key to almost all sightings.

Gas plasmas, or "ball lightning," are a little-understood natural phenomenon: lightning hits small, electrically charged regions of air, causing them to erupt into brightly burning globes. These glowing balls of burning gas can hover, cause car engines to stall, and even cause blips on radar screens.

Critics of this theory believe that gas

ALIEN EXPERT:
PHILIP J. KLASS

Philip Klass, a reporter for the technical magazine *Aviation Week*, has been debunking UFOs since 1966, when he wrote a scathing review of a book about a town undergoing a UFO flap. Klass concluded that the people were seeing ball lightning.

Since that time, Klass has gone on to become the premier UFO debunker, writing several books and magazine articles on the subject. He has been interviewed countless times on television, on the radio, and in print, promoting the skeptic's point of view on UFOs. Klass himself has backed away from the gas plasma theory as the explanation for most UFO sightings, and now suggests that all UFOs are hoaxes, misidentifications, or delusions.

plasmas could only be responsible for a small number of UFO sightings. Gas plasmas, they point out, last for a few seconds at most. They usually occur during thunderstorms and do not resemble metallic, disk-shaped crafts.

Man-Made Flying Saucers

Some ufologists believe that UFOs are man-made military prototypes of secret weapons. These researchers believe that the first flying saucers were really the inventions of the Germans in the last days of World War II.

According to this theory, German scientists built flying saucers capable of terrific speeds and fantastic maneuvers. After the war, the United States, England, and the Soviet Union gained hold of this technology. It has since been secret from the public as new weapons have been developed.

Space Critters

A theory first proposed during the 1950s suggests that UFOs are not spaceships, but actual creatures living in the atmosphere. These huge animals can materialize and disappear at will and maneuver at great speeds.

This theory was largely forgotten until the mid-1970s, when Trevor James Constable, a marine radio engineer, took infrared photographs of Earth's atmosphere. Constable believed he detected "amoeba-like life forms" living in the air. He theorizes that these "atmospheric animals" are made of fluids and gas with an electrical charge.

ALIEN FUN FACT: WHEN TO SEE UFOS

Statistically, your best chances to see a UFO are in the months of January, April, or October, between the hours of 9:00 p.m. and 10:00 p.m.

AUTOPSY OF A HOAX

During August of 1995, a "documentary" film titled *Alien Autopsy: Fact or Fiction?* was broadcast on television in the United States. The program included about twenty minutes of aged, grainy, black-and-white film purporting to show the autopsy of an alien being. If genuine, the footage was a priceless record of one of the most astounding events in human history.

The footage was discovered in 1992 by British television producer Ray Santilli. Santilli was in Cleveland, Ohio, looking for rare rock-and-roll film. While there, Santilli claims he met an elderly cameraman who offered to sell him some film he had shot in the Army. The cameraman told Santilli the film showed the autopsy of a dead alien

retrieved from the flying saucer crash at Roswell (p. 26).

Santilli went to the cameraman's home to see the footage. It was the most astonishing thing he had ever seen: a humanoid being, apparently a dead alien, lies on an operating table. A doctor cuts the creature's chest open and begins to remove unrecognizable organs. Santilli immediately realized how valuable the film was. After agreeing to share the profits with the cameraman, Santilli sold the film to TV networks around the world for millions of dollars.

Could the footage possibly be genuine? Or was it a blatant hoax?

The Skeptics Speak: Dummy Up

The Truly Dangerous Company, a Hollywood special-effects firm, has done an extensive analysis of Santilli's alien autopsy video. On the company's Web site (www.trudang.com), Trey Stokes—company co-founder and an expert puppeteer whose credits include The Abyss *and* Species—*posted an essay entitled "How to Make an Alien." Stokes convincingly explains why he believes the alien in the autopsy film is a fake.*

Trey and his team of effects experts observed the appearance of the alleged alien's flesh and the position of its shoulders, legs, and tensed muscles, discovering oddities that could only be explained if the alien were a rubber dummy. For instance, even though the creature is lying on its back on a table, its flesh seems to sag slightly toward its feet. This could be explained if the alien's body had been built from the mold of a human model who had been standing up when the mold was created. Gravity would have pulled the model's flesh toward the ground.

Stokes and his team also noted what they felt was suspicious behavior on the part of the doctors. Aside from opening the chest cavity of the alien, the doctors barely touch the creature. When one doctor peers into the alien's mouth, for instance, he doesn't even attempt to open the jaw. This is in contrast to an actual human autopsy, in which bodies need to be manipulated and moved in order to be examined. In Stokes's judgment, the "doctors" are really actors, handling a rigid model.

Other investigators have pointed out more problems with the film:

- It goes out of focus during important close-ups. Someone creating a hoax could use this lack of focus to hide giveaway details.

- Ray Santilli has never revealed the identity of the cameraman, and no independent reporter or researcher has ever been able to locate him.

- Several critics have pointed out that properly dissecting an alien would take months or years, not the hours this "autopsy" apparently took.

- Kodak has never examined the original negative to determine if the film stock was manufactured in 1947. According to a company representative, Kodak has made a standing offer to do so. So far, Ray Santilli has not taken Kodak up on this offer.

The Consensus

Not a single professional special-effects maker has stated a belief that the film is genuine. Almost as unanimous is the UFO community's response. With just a few exceptions, all the major voices in ufology agree the film is a hoax. This includes many ufologists who are still convinced that a flying saucer did crash near Roswell in 1947.

IF YOU SEE A UFO

You never know when you might see a flying saucer, so keep these tips in mind. UFO investigators rely on accurate, detailed sighting reports.

During the Sighting

- Stay calm. Remember that most UFOs turn out to have ordinary explanations, so chances are good you are not seeing anything extraordinary.
- Try to remember as much as you can about the object—its shape, color, distinguishing details, direction of travel, any sound it makes.
- Note how long the object is visible. How does the sighting end—does the object go behind a hill, move into the clouds, or simply disappear?
- If the object is moving, note whether it is heading in a straight line or making unusual moves or turns. Is it speeding, or floating slowly across the sky?
- If the object is moving in a straight line, you can help an investigator estimate its speed. When

the object passes over a stationary landmark, such as a tree, streetlight, or hill, time the object until it passes a second landmark.

- Determine how big the object is in the sky. To get an idea, hold up your thumb at arm's length. Does your thumb cover the object, or is the object bigger than your thumb? If the object is bigger, estimate whether the object would be covered by a baseball or a basketball held at arm's length.

- Determine the object's distance in relation to other objects in the sky or on the ground. For example, is the object above or below the clouds? Is it passing between you and a hill, or another stationary landmark?

- If the sighting takes place at night, note any other bright objects in the sky. This will later help investigators rule out stars and bright planets, such as Venus, which are often mistaken for UFOs.

- If other people are nearby, ask them if they can see the object, too. After the sighting, get their names and addresses so they can be contacted by UFO investigators.

Photographs and Videos

If you have a camera or camcorder handy during a sighting, don't hesitate to use it! But be prepared to have your photos or video met with skepticism. The vast majority of UFO photographs have proven to be hoaxes. If you follow a few precautions, however, your photos will get the attention they deserve.

If you believe you have taken a photograph of a UFO, do not take the film out of your camera. Do not touch the lens or change any of the settings on the camera, and do not rewind the film. Contact MUFON (p. 155) or another UFO organization immediately, and tell them that you believe you have a photo of a UFO on an unexposed roll of film in your camera. They will tell you what to do next.

If you have already had the film developed, be prepared to show the investigator the negatives of the entire roll along with your UFO photos. You have to be willing to show all the negatives, or the suspicion may arise that unconvincingly hoaxed pictures were left out. Your camera may also need to be examined.

A video of a UFO is even better than a photograph because it is much more difficult to convincingly fake. But it will still be subjected to intense scrutiny.

If the Sighting Becomes a CE2 or CE3

If the environment is affected during a UFO sighting or you actually see an alien, there are a few additional items to keep in mind.

If the object has left any noticeable effect on the surroundings, such as crushed or broken plants, a scorched area, landing-pad marks, or entity footprints, do not take or touch anything. Call MUFON or another UFO organization immediately and leave any investigation or sample collection to an experienced investigator.

If you have a camera with you and you can take photos of the traces without disturbing them, do so. If you see an alien outside a landed craft, don't panic. Unless the alien has come specifically to abduct you, chances are it will leave you alone. Witnesses report that most aliens encountered outside spacecraft generally seem to be involved in harmless activities, such as gathering plant and soil samples. When aliens become aware of being watched, they generally reenter their spaceship and take off.

After the Sighting

As soon as possible after a sighting, write down everything that happened, using as much detail as you can. Include all the information suggested above, and also add the following to your report:

- Where you were and what you were doing when you saw the object. Draw a simple map of the area where the sighting took place. Include landmarks such as trees, power lines, hills, etc. Note your position on the map, and also indicate the object's flight path. If the UFO landed, be sure to mark the location on your map. If you saw an alien, draw a sketch of the entity.
- How you first noticed the object.
- The time the sighting occurred.
- The weather conditions.
- What you were thinking or feeling when you saw the object.

Contact a UFO Investigator

When you have written everything down, contact a UFO investigator.

There are many reasons why you should report your sighting to an organization devoted to that purpose. For one thing, your report will ensure that accurate sighting statistics are recorded. For another, a UFO organization will be able to compare your report to other reports of the same object.

Finally, if your report is interesting enough, or if there are any landing traces or photographs, you may be contacted by an investigator from the group. They may want to interview you in person, or they may send you a detailed investigation report form to fill out. Your information may prove useful in solving the UFO mystery.

MUFON (Mutual UFO Network)

MUFON
103 Oldtowne Road
Seguin, TX 78155-4099
(www.mufon.com)
To report a UFO, call toll-free: 1-800-UFO-2166

MUFON (Mutual UFO Network) is the largest national organization devoted to investigating UFOs. Headquartered in Texas, they have offices in many states. Founded in 1969 by Walter H. Andrus, Jr., MUFON began with only a few investigators in the United States. It now has thousands of members worldwide, including scientists, doctors, and engineers in such disciplines as astronomy, psychology, and space technology.

If you are under the age of eighteen, you can join the organization as an associate member. Write to MUFON for more information.

CUFOS (J. Allen Hynek Center for UFO Studies)
CUFOS
2457 W. Peterson Avenue
Chicago, IL 60659
(www.cufos.org)

CUFOS (Center for UFO Studies) was founded in 1973 by J. Allen Hynek to help scientists and others investigate sightings and carry out research related to ufology. CUFOS maintains a massive library of UFO material and publishes books and magazines, including the *International UFO Reporter* and the scholarly *Journal of UFO Studies*.

After Hynek's death in 1986, the organization was renamed the J. Allen Hynek Center for UFO Studies.

National UFO Reporting Center
National UFO Reporting Center
P.O. Box 45623
University Station
Seattle, WA 98145
(www.ufocenter.com)
UFO Hotline: 1-206-722-3000

The National UFO Reporting Center was founded in 1974 with the object of keeping track of UFO-related sightings. The center also makes available summaries of all reported sightings.

The hotline is recommended for recent UFO sightings. Written reports of past sightings can be mailed to their address.

Intruders Foundation
Intruders Foundation
P.O. Box 30233
New York, NY 10011
(www.intrudersfoundation.org)

The Intruders Foundation was founded by abduction expert Budd Hopkins in 1990. If you believe you have had an abduction experience, or if you know someone who has, the Intruders Foundation can refer you to a trained mental-health professional in your area who can help.

The Skeptics Speak: CSICOP
CSICOP
Box 703
Amherst, NY 14226
(www.csicop.org)

CSICOP (the Committee for the Scientific Investigation of Claims of the Paranormal) encourages scientific scrutiny of extraordinary claims. The organization makes the results of its investigations available to the scientific community, the media, and the public. Their magazine, *The Skeptical Inquirer,* has printed articles debunking everything from sightings of Bigfoot and the Loch Ness monster to, of course, UFOs. Philip Klass is CSICOP's leading expert on UFO sightings.

Epilogue
LIFE IN A METEORITE

So what do you think?

Are we being visited by aliens?

Are people who see UFOs mistaken? Liars?

Or is there some other explanation that science has yet to discover?

While you ponder the question, consider this tantalizing thought:

In August 1996, NASA scientists announced the discovery of evidence suggesting that life had once existed on Mars. They found the controversial evidence in a meteorite labeled "Rock 84001" that struck an ice field in Antarctica thirteen thousand years ago. The chunk of rock had been flying through space for millions of years, ever since an ancient asteroid that collided with Mars knocked it from that planet's surface.

The scientists found in the meteorite molecules, or microscopic compounds, of a type often produced by living organisms. Additionally, when they looked at samples of the meteorite under powerful electron microscopes, scientists found objects that resembled fossilized single-celled creatures. The scientists found other tantalizing evidence of life in the meteorite as well.

This is far from proof of extraterrestrial life, and frankly, some scientists are skeptical. Taken individually, each piece of evidence found in the meteorite can be explained by other, non-living processes. However, because all of these clues appear together in one rock, it suggests that simple forms of life may have once existed on Mars. The discovery of life on any planet other than Earth—even primitive, one-celled creatures—would be one of the most important advances in the history of science.

However, some scientists are suggesting an even more astonishing theory. What if bacterial life from Mars had been brought to Earth on another meteorite billions of years ago? Such microbes might have been responsible for the beginning of life on our planet.

In which case, we might all be descendants of aliens!

Meteorite ALH84001 is believed to contain fossil evidence that life may have existed on Mars more than 3.6 billion years ago.

Far-Out:
A UFO Reading List

There are literally hundreds of books on UFOs and alien encounters. These are some of the best. If you want to read more on the subject of extraterrestrial life, this small selection is a good place to start. (Note that some may be out of print.)

History of UFOs

THE UFO ENCYCLOPEDIA by Jerome Clark (Omnigraphics, Inc., vol. 1, 1990; vol. 2, 1992; vol. 3, 1996). Jerome Clark has been investigating and writing about UFOs for three decades. This exhaustive and compulsively readable encyclopedia is the definitive UFO reference.

THE UFO EXPERIENCE: A SCIENTIFIC INQUIRY by J. Allen Hynek (H. Regnery Co., 1972). The book that introduced the world to the phrase "Close Encounters." Hynek tries to summarize all we know, and all we hope to find out, about UFOs.

THE UFO CONTROVERSY IN AMERICA by David Michael Jacobs (Indiana University Press, 1975). A thorough, thoughtful, and entertaining history of the UFO phenomenon and its effect on our society.

Roswell

THE TRUTH ABOUT THE UFO CRASH AT ROSWELL by Kevin Randle and Donald Schmitt (M. Evans and Co., 1994). Randle and Schmitt interviewed over one hundred witnesses of and participants in the Roswell incident and meticulously trace the chronology of events in this book. This is by far the most thorough work on the Roswell crash and its aftermath.

The Official Response

OUT THERE: THE GOVERNMENT'S SECRET QUEST FOR EXTRATERRESTRIALS by Howard Blum (Simon and Schuster, 1990). Is the government hiding what it knows about UFOs? This book, written by an investigative reporter, may convince you that the answer is yes.

THE REPORT ON UNIDENTIFIED FLYING OBJECTS by Edward J. Ruppelt (Doubleday, 1956). The first head of Project Blue Book gives his inside account of the Air Force's efforts to solve the UFO mystery.

MURMURS OF EARTH by Carl Sagan, et al. (Random House, 1978). This book tells the stories of the plaques that were attached to Pioneer 10 and 11 in 1972 and 1973, and the golden records attached to Voyager 1 and 2 in 1977. The author imagines what may happen if, far in the unimaginably distant future, extraterrestrial spacefarers find them.

5

Abductions

CLOSE ENCOUNTERS OF THE FOURTH KIND by C. D. B. Bryan (Knopf, 1995). Firsthand impressions of the Abduction Conference held at MIT in 1992.

THE INTERRUPTED JOURNEY by John Fuller (Dial Press, 1966). The gripping story of Betty and Barney Hill's abduction experience.

MISSING TIME and INTRUDERS by Budd Hopkins (Ballantine Books, 1982, 1987). These two best-sellers were the first to reveal the large numbers of people who were experiencing alien abductions.

ABDUCTION: HUMAN ENCOUNTERS WITH ALIENS by John E. Mack (Scribner's, 1994). A fascinating look at the abduction phenomenon by the Pulitzer Prize–winning former head of the Psychiatry Department at the Harvard Medical School.

High Strangeness

CIRCULAR EVIDENCE by Colin Andrews and Pat Delgado (Bloomsbury, 1989). The crop circle phenomenon described by its most experienced investigators. Filled with beautiful and intriguing photographs.

THE MONUMENTS OF MARS by Richard Hoagland (North Atlantic Books, 1987). The mystery of The Face on Mars as explained by its leading investigator.

Alternate Theories
DIMENSIONS and REVELATIONS by Jacques Vallee (Ballantine Books, 1988, 1991). Two important books by perhaps the most respected authority on the subject of UFOs.

Skeptics
UFOS EXPLAINED by Philip J. Klass (Random House, 1974). The top UFO debunker offers ordinary explanations for some of the most extraordinary UFO sightings.

WATCH THE SKIES! by Curtis Peebles (Smithsonian Institution Press, 1994). An encyclopedic, skeptical look at the flying saucer "myth."

Acknowledgments

Many, many thanks to Amy Freeman, my "out of
this world" research assistant. May the Force
always be with her.

I owe a special debt of gratitude to my editor,
Alice Jonaitis, whose patience is as infinite as
space itself, and whose knowledge of the arcane
art of editorial alchemy enabled her to
transmute my leaden prose into poetry.

—E.E.

Index